W9-DFK-991

How to Marry a Minister

HOW TO MARRY A MINISTER

by Martha Hickman

J. B. Lippincott Company
Philadelphia and New York

"I Learn to Speak Methodist," "We'll Be Home Tomorrow," and part of "Parsonages Proper" have appeared in *Christian Herald*. "What Does Your Husband Do?" has appeared in abridged form in *The Pulpit*. "Parsonages Proper" was originally entitled "An Attic Is Forever."

To the one I did

An Admittedly Defensive Introduction to
a Book about Ministers' Family Life

Why, in this year of our Lord, a book about ministers' family life? For those of us who live out our lives being wives of ministers, this is in one way a strange question. It *is* our life, we know it is authentic life, and is not authentic life what books are about, whether one is a minister or a baseball player or a psychiatrist? One may as well ask, Why another book about people? So, as a book about authentic life, I, who happen to be married to a minister, write this book.

What else? For it is I who has asked the question, and defensively, too. Why a book about a minister's family, and not a radical book at that? The "in" thing in religion today is to soft-pedal what is conventional, to play a sort of me-first game in which churchmen denigrate the church and themselves for not being relevant. I think it does make us uneasy from time to time that, being committed to a view of life that is so radical, we nonetheless find ourselves conforming to so many of the conventions of society—raising our children, attending the services of the church, enjoying our homes and our families—in a world that is torn apart. We tell ourselves that healing for the world's chaos may come from the strengths of families like ours, free enough in their own security before God to reach out in love to others. And then we tell ourselves again, because the specter of sackcloth and ashes does not go easily away.

But do we ever think, we who are very close to the church, that though our lives are in some ways conventional, they are not —to use that magic word today—"relevant"? Not for a second! For if God is not to be found here, in the deepest relationships in which human beings are bound to one another—in the luminous moment, the comic aside, the uproar and grief and thanksgiving of families—we know He cannot be found at all, in any way that matters very much. This affirmation, too, is part of my message here, and it seems a good word to speak in a time of upheaval.

So, here it is—this book about the family life of a minister of the church. Will anyone but the in-group really care? (A *priest's* family might be a provocative subject of public light in this New Day, but a *minister's* family?)

I hope the in-group does care, and I think they will understand both the uneasiness and the affirmation. They number enough to be a gratifying audience for any book. I am one of them—their sister, the in-law of their husbands, the wife of one of the ministers of their church. So, in order to celebrate for these in the family some of the aspects of the high and low drama of the life we share, I write this book.

I have another hope, and it is a faint one, but, happily, it will not die. That is the hope that in this book there may be enough authentic life that some person of open and sensitive spirit, who has turned with sorrow away from a religion he thought was a sober and constricting affair, may perk up his ear and with a hopeful heart turn and look again, and may even find among the people of God some prospect of good company for the road.

Martha Hickman

Erie, Pennsylvania, 1968

Acknowledgments

Having no research team or professional associates to whom I owe particular acknowledgment, I would, nonetheless, like to express my gratitude to the following persons:

To Kenneth Wilson, for his encouragement and his belief in me as a writer, in the days when I wondered whether this secondary vocation was going to work out at all;

To my parents, George and Ruth Whitmore, for life, for the long outpouring of love and nurture, for a good education, for an inheritance of New England integrity, a sense of humor, and, I hope, the grace of an inquiring mind;

To my parents-in-law, Leon and Mayme Hickman, for the kind of love and support no daughter-in-law has a right to expect, and which gives the back of the hand to all jokes about in-laws;

To my children, for sharing my interest in this project and for giving their permission to become, to the extent that they do here, objects of public view;

To my husband, for technical assistance, for reading my pages, for encouraging me with constant love and occasional suggestions, and for being unwilling for me to stop with any chapter before I had what I wanted;

And to all others who find themselves on the pages of this book, for their share in the action.

Contents

How to Marry a Minister

I
How to Marry a Minister
in the First Place

*(If you are already married to a minister and just
want to know how to make the best of it,
you can skip this chapter)*

Believe it or not, Ripley, there are young women whose matri-
monial aim is to marry a minister. Not a particular minister, at
least not at first. But someone in the profession. I knew such a
young woman once. She said to me, "I've always thought I'd *love*
to marry a minister." Our friendship, begun at a summer conference, did not blossom. I could not understand such thinking.

Here I am, married to a minister. And she? I do not know.
She indicated to me at the time, though, that she was not alone—
she had lots of friends who also wanted to marry ministers.

So I know there are such people, and I would like to suggest
to them, from my vast experience of having married one minister, and unsystematically at that, some likely ways to proceed.

One obvious plan if you want to marry a minister is to latch on to someone who is thinking of becoming a minister and stick with him. This will at least assure that you are in on the ground floor, before any vocational glamour increases his desirability to others who are also looking for minister husbands. But you should know from the beginning that you are in for a long haul before your intended husband, if he goes through with it, completes his education and can start practicing his ministering. Education for ministers today means four years of college and at least three of seminary, and you will have to decide whether it is worth all this time of being either the actual or intended wife of a minister-to-be in order to, at the end of the time, be married to a minister. By sticking with a medical student this long you could be married to an almost-doctor and have a much higher expected annual income in the years ahead. Or be married to a college teacher and become enmeshed in the stimulus and cross-winds of faculty life and hobnob with visiting writers and scientists instead of visiting bishops and missionaries. Though you might prefer bishops and missionaries to writers and scientists anyway. But ministerial education is a long process and you should be prepared to defer your goal for a number of years, perhaps even to support your husband partially as he wends his way through courses on Economics for Christians and Hermeneutics II.

Furthermore, if you seize the earliest opportunity of marrying someone who is "planning to be a minister," his plans may change, and you may find yourself married to a teacher or an engineer instead. Almost anyone of humanitarian bent who is not downright hostile to the church has at one time or another "thought of being a minister." So if you team up with such a person in the expectation that he will see it through and you will then be married to a minister, you may be in for a big surprise. A lot of people think of exploring the Arctic, but not many go through with it. Of course there are ascertainable degrees of intention, and in your earliest conversations with a possible minister you should find out whether he is seriously planning to be a minister or just giving himself the luxury of some church-related altruistic thoughts. But be subtle about your inquiries. No one, prospective minister or industrial heir, likes to think he is of interest for reasons other than himself. If you suggest going to church on three dates in a row and he concurs, assume he is religiously insecure and will never be a minister; if he suggests a movie or a play after the first or second date, and has exhibited some church interest before, he is worth cultivating as a possible future minister. But at this early stage, his vocational future is still a gamble, and you are running a very big risk that his "plans" to become a minister will run aground long before he reaches his first baptismal font.

A safer procedure is to start looking for a future minister husband among the ranks of students in divinity schools. Even this is no sure thing. While chances are certainly higher that a divinity school student will turn into a minister than that a high-minded Boy Scout or high school or college student who is "thinking of becoming a minister" will turn into one, enough divinity students somewhere along the way decide to become physicists or teachers or salesmen that you might end up married to one of these. One fellow student of my husband in divinity school decided shortly before his graduation that his vocation was to be not a minister but a psychiatrist—which, if his wife had married him with any fond intention of being a minister's wife, she would need one of before they were through. But it is probably worth the risk of his changing to something else to look for a future minister husband among the ranks of divinity school students.

Here, too, though, there are more and less prudent ways to proceed. You could settle in a town where there is a divinity school and try to get a job in the library or bookstore. But these jobs are usually in great demand by the wives of students already married and helping support their husbands, and, the administration having a vested interest in keeping these students solvent enough to continue in school, the wives will probably have first chance at the jobs. This is not fair, as you need the exposure more than the wives do, but it is one of the facts of graduate school life.

If the divinity school is part of a university complex, you may decide to enroll at one of the other graduate schools—say, the school of hospital administration or the graduate school of archaeology—and hope reciprocal social occasions will throw you with divinity students. They may, but then again they may not, and this is, at best, a rather long shot. But if you find studying hospital administration or archaeology a rather appealing prospect in itself the course is certainly worth considering, though it may result in your marrying a hospital administrator or an archaeologist and not a minister at all.

The best way to meet a prospective minister husband, of course, if you can swing it, is to enroll in divinity school as a fellow student. You do not have to take the full treatment to qualify yourself to become a minister; this takes a lot of courage for women, not to mention academic ability, not to mention the funds necessary to finance a full three-year course. (Some seminaries and churches offer generous scholarships for ministerial students, but these usually go to the men, whose image as future clergymen is more convincing than yours would be—unless you wish to dress in drab clothes and effect a kind of feminine sackcloth-and-ashes role, in which case you are not too likely to marry a minister at all. Despite the common image of ministers and ministerial students as being concerned about things of the spirit, it is interesting to note how in most cases the handsomest ministers end up with the best-looking wives, thus including in the equation of minister marriages the same factors that operate in marriages of football players and other folk-hero types.)

Consider enrolling in divinity school, then, not as a candidate for the full ministerial degree but as a candidate for the degree in religious education. This takes two years after college instead of three and is less threatening to the public mind, including the mind of the male divinity student, than for a girl to be studying to be a minister. Of course it still takes some courage, for reasons hereafter explained, and academic ability, and the necessary funds. But if you should succeed, against your better judgment, in going through the full two-year course and acquiring a degree in religious education instead of a minister husband, you will find that qualified religious educators are in high demand and short supply. While you continue to watch out of the corner of your eye for possible husband candidates, you can pursue your interim vocation as a religious educator at a higher salary and in a more sophisticated setting than if you were a more extensively trained lady minister.

About the need for courage in enrolling in divinity school— everyone will think he has the goods on you, and you may become sensitive to all the remarks to the effect that what you are really doing in school is looking for a husband. The best response to such heckling is to ignore it. If you concur you will jeopardize your chances; if you vehemently disagree you will be accused of protesting too much. Affect a Mona Lisa smile and let the inferences pass.

You will get this reaction to your choice of graduate school not only from the world at large, however, but from the male students in the school as well, though they probably will not say so to your face. But you will get the message of their avowed disinterest in women fellow students as possible future wives. For one thing, such a woman would know too much of the field in which her husband is supposed to be the expert. For another, familiarity breeds contempt or, to put it another way, "With Harvard men who know Radcliffe best it's Wellesley two to one." With these home-based skeptics of your motives and position in school do not be alarmed. Such an attitude on the part of male divinity students is purely a defensive maneuver and will not stand up under the eroding influence of a really wise candidate for a degree in religious education.

Now—which students to aim for? Among the male not-already-married students at divinity school the most likely to cooperate with your desire to become a minister's wife are those midway through their third year. This is the time when "third-year panic" sets in. The students see the date of graduation advancing. They envision themselves at last as practicing ministers, ensconced in glorious authority as sensitive adequate pastors of local congregations. But—to whom will they turn when their sensitivity is rubbed raw, their authority questioned, their adequacy in doubt, if not to their parish at least to themselves? And that parsonage—how are they going to manage that? Who will share the responsibility of absorbing the ladies' enthusiasm for all bazaars, suppers, and other good works? And who will protect the minister from the wiles of predatory females whose eagerness to marry any bachelor minister has been part of the in-group repartee for at least three years of divinity school education? Who indeed? It is when this third-year panic is at its height that male divinity students who have held out stalwartly against the wiles of lady students are apt to conclude that a theologically trained wife may be an asset after all and that, God's plan for life including the desire for marriage on the part of women as well as men, there is nothing so gauche about a girl's going to divinity school with mixed motives. Now is the time to be on hand, and all of your labors through the Old Testament prophets and your fine refutations of the Pelagian Heresy will seem to have been worthwhile.

It should be said that there are young women who enroll in divinity schools not because they want to marry a minister but because they want—genuinely want—to be religious educators or even ministers. Their motives will be suspect by all fellow students, male and female, as well as by all other single ladies who want to marry ministers and who resent the inside track they know fellow students must have. This resentment and suspicion will be hard to take, but a lady minister will just have to stand the gaff, realizing her trials are as nothing compared to those of Luther or even St. Teresa, and pursue her determined course, from which, who knows, some divinity student, seized with third-year panic and the desires of springtime and youth, may, against her original intention, rescue her. At this time everyone will gather around and say, "I told you so," but by then she will not much care.

If marrying someone who is "planning to be a minister" seems just too risky, and if enrolling in a graduate divinity school seems too long and expensive a grind, you can always wait and take your chances on one of the few ministers who reach their first parish in an unmarried state. But you will have stiff competition. Not only will various other young single women look upon the unmarried minister as eligible, but so will middle-aged widows and others to whom the lonely-and-good image conjured up by the single minister presents a special appeal.

Besides, how many young attractive single ministers do you know? I know one—in a city of 150,000. Of course I know a lot of attractive Catholic priests. But they are not—at least not yet—considered fair game. And anyone who would want to marry a minister is likely to have scruples against that drastic a change in religion. A Baptist to a Methodist is one thing; a Baptist to a Catholic is a fish of a different water.

II
What Does Your Husband Do?

Moving around from city to city, finding my way among the various civic and cultural groups to which I may be attracted and in which my husband's vocation is not already known, I find, over many a juggled coffee cup and crumpled paper napkin, a peculiar moment of truth as I am asked again and again the question, "And what does *your* husband do?"

The answer is easy. "He is a minister." But then the small breezes of reaction begin to stir.

Before I had been asked this question many times I began to discern certain ways in which my answer was met. There is the quick, flat "Oh, I see," which relegates the minister to a nice harmless pasturage among conventional and staid groups of people who preserve a timid and irrelevant status quo. There is the reaction of veiled hostility to or at least impatience with the church on the part of people who were perhaps overdosed with institutionalized "churchism" in their childhood and have looked elsewhere for significant orientation of their life and values. There is the too-enthusiastic gush of the person for whom ministry carries some kind of ennobling nimbus which, by setting the minister apart, may also make him ineffective as a contingent force on real problems but venerable nonetheless. There is also, of course, the response of honest interest in this as one stimulating and important fact about a new acquaintance, and perhaps the expectation that with this new acquaintance a meaningful conversation may at some time ensue.

I, the minister's wife, with coffee cup in hand and weather vane whirling, playing out my own set of counterresponses (showing that I am up on Edward Albee and Happenings, on Freudian psychology; that I too am disenchanted with the shortcomings of the church, exercising my sharp sense of humor), may wonder at times what these things add up to and may wish that for the good of all some more discerning image of ministry would be communicated than that of someone who, by a kind of divine fiat, preaches and prays, counsels and teaches, goes—if he is really far out—on an occasional freedom march, and may break into "secular" life occasionally by taking the neighborhood boys fishing or lending a limited sanctity to civic occasions. (How many times have I, pushing my loaded—we have four children—cart around the supermarket, been greeted cordially by a parishioner who says, half in jest and half in earnest, "You have to eat, too!" as though it is a bit surprising that we have to do such ordinary things as restock periodically at the grocery store.)

"He is a minister." Well, what about it? What shapes the kind of fuzzy outline most people seem to have of what being a minister means today? Is it a realistic outline? Does it look the same to the minister as to the man outside? Does the shape differ today from, say, a hundred or even fifteen years ago? How, here, does the shape look to the minister's wife? What really gives the ministry its meaning?

There are some technical particulars associated with the church which are sometimes thought to be distinctive, but they are not peculiar to the ministry at all. A minister, particularly in some denominations, moves around every several years: so do engineers, so do servicemen, so do certain levels of personnel in most of America's large corporations. The minister is associated closely with the institution of the church: so are men in other professions associated with the institutions they work for—a bank, a factory, a college—and the intergroup relations in these institutions are probably no less subject to tension than are those of the church, although we seem to expect people in church to act without the pettiness and selfishness they carry around with them wherever they go. A minister tends to be lionized or criticized by groups of the people he works with: so do other men in the institutions of which they are leaders.

What is there today, in this age of science and revolution, that validates to a man the calling of being a minister—and to his wife, who faces the mixed chorus of public reaction to her husband's vocation plus the queries of her own mind, and who is perhaps in a position to appreciate its frustrations more clearly than its gifts?

As the church has slipped from its high place, so has the status of the clergy slipped. The minister today speaks from no platform of common consent. He is assumed to have no undemonstrated relevance; he receives no automatic hearing. To the extent that this fall in status disturbs us, perhaps to that extent we do not understand the possibilities and nature of ministry at all. Maybe we had the wrong assumptions about ministry, and the "fall in status" has been a necessary concomitant to a more honest view of what the vocation of minister really is. Perhaps the things a minister of today really values in his work were no easier to achieve in the days of a more prestigious clergy. Do we feel that the minister is no longer able to command the loyalty and attention of a large group? When was he ever, by some magic of his presence, able to affect in any meaningful way large groups of otherwise uncommitted persons? Does a lawyer expect such disproportionate returns on the labors of his hand and mind? Does a researcher, who may contribute to radical changes by some of his work, but who may spend years of his life without producing immediately useful result? Does a teacher? Does a homemaker? A minister has as much time and personal power at his disposal as do most other men. If a man ever thought of the ministry as somehow enabling him magically to multiply the effects of his labor, surely he can no longer sustain such an unrealistic image; perhaps now he can more wisely weigh the various real components of his calling.

If society gives him less authority than he once had in one respect, in another respect he may wish it would give him less. I refer to the concept of the minister as an "answer man"—the assumption that somehow the minister, by virtue of his position, is secure in the face of insecurities that threaten other people, fearless in the face of other people's fears, as some people may feel that if they had a doctor in the family they need never be sick. No one knows better than a minister how far from reality this is. Presumably he has a basic faith in the Christian gospel or he would not be a minister. But he has no more magic access to God or private vision of His will than other people have. He may have more time and interest in studying about faith, he may have more demanding confrontations with tragedy and in that sense be forced to work out some viable way of meeting these things, but his Bible has no extra pages, the air in his study is filled with no special voices proclaiming God's reality, and his familiarity with holy things may at times endanger rather than support his religious sensitivities. I have heard my husband describe the position of the minister in regard to any "answer man" qualities in this way: "We are all travelers in a labyrinth—I as well as you. I am no taller than you, to see above the pattern, to see where the end will come out. I do not stand on high hill beside the labyrinth, freed of its uncertainties and able to tell you from my high ground what the labyrinth is certainly like. I have reason to believe this is how it is, but such conviction and faith as I have, such sense of its patterns as I have, come to me in this labyrinth, too." So, if he dares, the minister may bear witness to his own need of support, of his own reliance on the upholding of the community of the people of God, and may join with his people in urging them to cast aside any image of him as a holder by proxy of the faith they wish they had, so that together they may really know the meaning of the commandment: "Thou shalt have no other Gods before me."

Nor is a "spiritual quality" any more easily acquired by a minister and his family than it would be by any other family. I am reminded of once reading that some women are attracted to ministers as prospective husbands because they anticipate a sort of spiritual, minimally sexual marriage; at the time I did not see how such a marriage could be considered attractive or even truly a marriage at all. A minister's family life, or his own, assumes no "spiritual" quality by virtue of his vocation. Hopefully, it is a deeply perceptive life, but so is the life of any sensitive, honest person. In being a minister (or a minister's wife!) there is no guarantee of being a person of unshakable faith, free from dark nights, loneliness, or misgiving, any more than the ancient Hebrews were protected against personal and community disaster because they named the name of God.

If neither society-endowed power—power for good, but power nonetheless—nor unshakable faith, nor a kind of "spiritualized" perception of reality validates a minister's vocation, what, aside from his denomination's requirements and his professionally acquired skills, gives him "license to preach," both from the pulpit and as he acts out his ministry through pastoral work, community involvement, study, prayer, and all the rest? Aside from being the agent of an institution that he believes *can* be a power for good (as opposed, for instance, to being a dope pusher, which is hard to justify from almost any moral position), he must have a sense of himself as carrying out his vocation in a *primary arena* —of dealing through the tools of his total life and ability with issues and events of first importance: the meaning or meaninglessness of life, the search for identity, the prospect of personal continuity, the meaning of community. Even the repudiation of faith is a question of faith. Even the denial of any overarching values is a question of faith. Certainly matters of legal and political judgment are matters of faith. The fact that a man sees ministry as a primary arena is part of his calling to be a minister, his sense that this is where God wants him to use his life. There will be people who do not agree with him that ministry is a primary arena, who will think that science or education or politics is the *real* place where "the action is" today, but this is part of their calling to be—and their security in being—scientists, educators, or politicians.

A man may take his place in various parts of the arena of ministry. We read references to the "new breed" of ministers, committed to a public ministry, who participate heavily in freedom marches, who lobby for better housing opportunities for minority groups, who, as ministers, become students of sociology or psychology, proclaiming that God lives most fully through the secular institutions of culture. For such a minister, this is his part of the arena.

Or he may take his primary place as a pastor, incorporating into his life such elements of public ministry as he feels will be most helpful to his work as a pastor and to his life as a Christian. It is not easy to choose to be a pastor today. Even in the church, pastoral work has fallen into some disrepute. Pastoral counselors are disposed of as "the last of the pietists," as persons to talk with "if you can't afford a psychiatrist." Pastors are the people who stay on the farm, while their brothers with greater gumption and insight go to the big city or the college to become organizers of the disinherited or teachers of new theories of religion.

But beyond all the new waves of whatever the new sea is about this time—child labor yesterday, better housing today; higher criticism yesterday, the Essene influence today—a man who is a pastor garners to himself the support of the historical church, the support of the rituals of the present-day church by which he himself is sustained, the privilege which society, realizing the deep needs of people in the prospect or presence of anguish, gives to him, and he goes among his people as a shepherd, as a priest, as a comforter, as a friend. And as he goes among his people, not as an answer man but as a fellow human being, the overtones of his known allegiance to the church, the stance of his life, do give him a presence more than his own, a support more affirming, more hopeful, more reassuring, than if he came as an unaligned friend. I think of a professor at divinity school, speaking of his own need for a pastor, saying, "I want someone to stand with me before God." Perhaps it is here, as a man stands with his people before God, that he discovers the true nature of pastoral ministry —not in some over-all rationale, sociologically defensible, but here among the least of these (and who stands before God except as one of the least of these?), when reality stands in the room like sunlight, or like snow on the ground, when a minister becomes an artist-participant, a dealer in the particular, not a theoretician at all.

"What does your husband do?" As I wonder about the image of the clergyman today, knowing how chimerical are the securities of faith sometimes ascribed to my husband and me because he is a minister and I am a minister's wife, I realize that for all my sometime protest there *is* a special security in being a minister's wife: it is the security for me of being associated this closely with what is to me, also, a primary arena, and of being this close to a mediator of help when I too, as I so often do, need "someone to stand with me before God."

As I see my husband come home night after night from evening meetings and calling, as we plan his time off so carefully for the family's best benefit because, except for our lovely summer vacations, there is so little of it, as I recognize that society does not hold the pastoral ministry in marvelously high regard these days and that other professions cut a wider swath in the intellectual and academic world to which we sometimes feel so drawn, as I wonder what our life would be like were he the lawyer or professor he so easily might have become, and as these small voices speak like a crowd and I realize my own need for reassurance that this splendidly able, perceptive, and sensitive man is doing what he should with his vocational life and power, I think, Where else—from what other platform—could he deal so effectively with what matters most to him? And I think, too, of those words of Blanche DuBois: "Sometimes there's God so quickly."

"And what does your husband do?"

"He is a minister."

I think of him going at the request of a mutual friend to visit a stranger who was fatally ill. When he came home he told me about it. "When I first got there, he was very bitter," he said. "His experience with the church had been unhappy. He would rather I had not intruded."

"Was your visit helpful?"

"I think so." He thought awhile and then said, "The privilege society gives us ministers—I wouldn't have had the *gall*. . . ." Several days later the man was admitted to the hospital and my husband went again to see him. That evening he said, "He told me he'd been bitter the other day, but he was glad now that I had come. He said, 'I need all the help I can get.'" How different death might have been for this man had he not had a minister to "stand with him" through his last days.

I think of a man in mid-life whose wife told me one day that because of his association with my husband he had stopped drinking at a point which his doctor later described as just in time to avoid serious physical damage. I doubt whether my husband even knew alcohol was a problem for this particular parishioner—we hadn't known each other very long—but we had been through together one of those harrowing in-group fusses which seem to plague certain small churches from time to time, and we had come out the other side of it with a renewed sense of what Christian fellowship really is. I remember the man standing in the doorway of our home one day and saying, as he was about to leave, "We have something here we didn't have before. And I didn't think it would happen so soon."

I think of driving my husband to a protest march against the killing of James Reeb in Selma, Alabama, which our community, along with many others in the nation, was holding the Sunday afternoon after that tragic week. As we got near the place where the marchers were to assemble, the traffic got so thick that we were just barely moving and my husband said, suddenly, "Oh, there's Jerry. Let me out here and I'll go the rest of the way with him." I stopped the car and he got out, called, "Hey, Jerry!" and I saw one of the young priests of our city stop and turn toward us. "Hi, Hoyt!" he said, and waited, and they walked off together, their heads inclined in conversation. I thought of how in this city until a few years ago, and in the city in which I had grown up, Protestant and Catholic clergymen had hardly even nodded to each other except at the City Hall steps on Memorial Day.

I think of him learning that a woman he had talked with many times in her sickness and despondency had, a few hours after his last visit with her, taken an overdose of medicine and killed herself, leaving for him a note hoping God would forgive her.

I think of him happily spending many hours with college students, helping them find their way to an intellectually viable faith in a world bursting with questions.

I think of him standing on the sidewalk talking to a man of subnormal intelligence, an acquaintance of only several moments, finding something to talk about and acknowledging as much dignity in that man as he would were he in conversation with the most erudite of scholars.

I think of him going at midnight to pick up a young man he has known before who has called him from a pay station downtown—he has just been released from jail and he can't go home because his parents won't take him in—and spending the major part of the next several days helping this young man find a job and a place to live, trying to restore some trust between the young man and his father.

I think of him standing by the baptismal font with a young couple who, after years of childlessness and of the wife's precarious health, have brought their baby daughter to be baptized.

"What does your husband do?"

"He is a minister."

The phone rings in the middle of the night. It is by the bed and I answer it, groggily. The voice is one I know, rasping and hurried because there's no time to talk. "Martha, tell Hoyt I think Mother's dying." "I'll tell him, Anna." She has already hung up.

I turn to him and tell him, and he gets up and dresses and is gone into the night, to the sure face of death. I lie and think, If it were *my* mother. I think of Anna and the crochety complaining woman who has been her mother and who now is dying, and I pray for them, holding them in a love I do not fathom whose name is God, but as tenaciously as the grip of a claw, and I pray for myself as well and for all human beings who in daylight or in the middle of some near or distant night come upon the great mystery of death and, all speculation suddenly irrelevant, all musings and secondhand experiencing gone, know this time it is for them.

In a while my husband comes home. "She was dead before I got there, or the doctor, either," he says.

I nod. "How is Anna?" I ask, perhaps for curiosity, perhaps for reassurance. I hope for love.

"About as you'd expect," he says. About as you'd expect. As I'd expect of myself. My heart goes out to her—down three blocks and around a corner—and I live with her there, trying to uphold her. Some human love, that's all I can offer her, some love to hold her. And I think of what it means to me, that my husband is a minister.

"I want someone to stand with me before God."

"And what does your husband do?"

"He is a minister."

III
With the Children

I suppose all children play doctor and nurse and, in their early youth, variations on the junkman and construction-worker themes. But our children have affinities for minister play.

For what distinguishes ministers' children from other children is not the things that used to set them apart—that they don't go to movies and dances (our children do) or that they do go to every activity the church offers for their age group (our children do not). What distinguishes ministers' children from other children is that their in-group allusions are minister's-family allusions, their in-group jokes are minister's-family jokes. At the age of five John builds an "altar" in the snow in the front yard. Household staples of canned peaches and pears become "canned preachers" and "canned prayers." A black witch's costume can as easily be a clerical robe for use in conducting imaginary services. Peter, trying to get permission to watch an extra television show on Sunday afternoon which promises to be more violent than his mother's leftover childhood feelings about appropriate Sunday activities can easily accept, says, "But it's very churchy

—it's called 'Arizona *Mission*' "—or, as we discuss a family which has been undecided for a year about whether or not to join the church, sings a parody of a cigarette commercial, "Come on over to the chur-urch side."

Because their father is a minister our children have a security about matters of religion which permits parodies other children might not allow themselves and other parents might not feel free to enjoy. A particularly extreme opportunistic-evangelical radio program, in which business success and a return to health always accompany religious conversion, is referred to by the children as "the horror show." A faith healer given to bizarre claims (that a runny nose is the sign of "the devil coming out!") sends them reeling from the television room clutching their stomachs in laughter.

Their participation in church services is different, too. They are connoisseurs at an early age of ministerial speech types. A visiting preacher may have "too many ah's and uh's." A visit to a church of which an uncle, given to a personal, informal style, is minister, brings the comment from Mary, "I think I understand Uncle Willis' sermons—he kept saying, 'When I was a boy.'" Misprints in the words of bulletins are good for pokes and smiles. A slip of the tongue sends John's head ducking in mock embarrassment. An allusion to anything that has happened in our family ("My children gave me a book for Father's Day called *Two Thousand Insults for All Occasions*") sends a conspiratorial smile down the row of us, sitting together in the pew. In a rare flight into extravagant personal memorabilia, Hoyt says, one Sunday when candles and flowers are out in full array, "The experience we had together kindled a flame in my life that has never gone out," and Peter, observing the candles precariously dripping leeward in the breeze, mutters under his breath, "You can say that again!" Or Stephen, listening to an Old Testament reading with particularly harrowing details, whispers in half-earnest horror, "What talk!"

We have friends coming to visit us. They are Quakers, members of the Society of Friends. Like some Friends and unlike others, they use the old form of address—thee and thy—when speaking to each other. So that the children will not be astonished at this unusual form of address, we tell them our friends will speak this way, and they can be prepared. They are charmed. There ensues a lengthy conversation among the children. "Will thee pass the bread?" "Will thee get thy clumsy foot off my chair?" "Will thee excuse me if I knock thy head off?" and other examples of gracious conversation. They are hilarious. After they have sobered down a bit, they ask what Quakers believe different from what we believe. We describe their originally different form of worship—that in their pure form they do not have ministers, that they conduct their meetings for worship in silence but that people speak when they feel moved to speak. The children are charmed again. One of them rises and begins to intone, "I am moved to say—" Another one quavers, "Don't speak. Don't speak," pleadingly. The others take turns at rising. "I am moved to say that I am great." "I am moved to say that you are a bunch of clods." And so it goes. This may not be the ideal introduction to comparative religion, but at least it is honest, fun, and free from false piety. When our friends have come and the children of both families have gone to bed for the night, we recount our previous discussion, and when we get to the dramatic pleas of "Don't speak," the father of the family says, "I feel that way myself often enough." It is good fun and we understand each other.

Nor do their views of some parts of the church's program carry any overtones of undeserved reverence. John is contemplating the coming session of Bible school. This is the last summer he is eligible to go, and he would happily skip this one. "Bible school!" he sputters. "Paper churches and messy salt maps and Kool-Aid and crumbly cookies!" He does go, and enjoys it, but he and Stevie are not above parodying the girls doing an interpretive dance to "Fairest Lord Jesus"—waving their arms and swooping from dining-room chair to living-room sofa. Or Peter plays back a tape he has made on the family tape recorder: "Happiness is not having to go to Sunday school." But then Peter goes to no end of trouble working with a friend on a special act for the youth fellowship show, and John comes home from a church youth council meeting, to which he went as an elected representative, with new confidence in himself and pleasure in the evening of discussion and listening to records.

The children have planned a wedding of dolls. It is Mary's idea, but she has been promised cooperation by John and Stephen. Peter would not miss out on the occasion but must preserve his condescending distance. Each of the children has a small troll doll, and the wedding which Mary is going to stage is to marry her troll and Stevie's. I think this is the third wedding we have had—always at Mary's suggestion—for this domesticating species. Mary's and Stevie's trolls were married a couple of years ago. Then, alas, Stevie, being unused to the necessity of not putting anything down in a public spot in New York City, lost his at the World's Fair. A wedding of its successor was arranged to Mary's troll, Maria, and happiness again prevailed. Then Mary left

Maria in a restroom on the New York Throughway, and her successor was in time acquired. Nothing would do but we must have another wedding of the new Maria and Stevie's troll, Sam. John has agreed that he, in the person of his troll, will be the officiating minister and also that he, being the accomplished pianist among the children, will play the piano.

The wedding is set for Sunday afternoon at three o'clock, and several of Mary's friends promise to be on hand for the ceremony. About Thursday I become caught up in the excitement and, with school looming in a few weeks, knowing there will be much less chance for family foolishness, get into the act by baking a wedding cake. The cake is a marvelous baroque affair, made to Mary's wishes—three layers, small on top and graduating to about a five-inch-square base at the bottom layer, with white frosting and ribbons and flowers of pink frosting decoration. The friends gather around to admire the cake and make elaborate engineering plans as to its cutting and who is to get which corner, and we put the cake in the freezer until Sunday.

At the appointed hour on Sunday Mary has her troll, Maria, dressed in wedding finery. Stevie's troll, Sam, is encased in a black felt suit. Mary's friends arrive. A friend of Peter's shows up, unaware that he is about to witness anything special. He and Peter are shown to places they may sit and warned sternly by Mary that they are not to clown around. Peter's friend, Tom, keeps shaking his head and saying, "I don't believe it. I don't believe it." Mary tells the other spectators where they are to sit. Stevie, who by now is a bit embarrassed to be a participant in the exaggerated romanticism, staggers his troll around the wedding locale (a designated space of carpet) with many asides expressing reluctance at getting married. ("Oops, excuse me, but I don't

want to get married. Stumble, stumble. Fall on face," and so on.)
John discovers that his troll, who is to be the minister, is without
clothing. A minor scurry shows up nothing suitable for him to
wear, so John wraps the troll's long blue hair around his body
and announces he is ready. Someone sings:

> "When Father goes in swimming no swimming suit for him,
> He wraps his whiskers 'round him, and then he plunges in."

Mary shouts, "Begin, John! Begin! Play the wedding march!"

John goes to the piano, makes a couple of false starts on "Chop-
sticks" and "Do-Re-Mi," and then plonks out the opening bars
of "The Wedding March." Peter leaps to his feet, wraps the
afghan around himself, and shouts, "*I'll* be the minister!"

"No, no!" Mary says. "You'll wreck it. *John* is the minister."
Peter returns to his seat beside Tom. John moves from the piano
bench to man his blue-hair-wrapped "minister" in front of Sam
and Maria. John gives his version of the vows.

"Do you, Sam, promise to be faithful to your wife, Maria, in
sickness and in health, in richer and in poorer, and in any other
type situation?"

"Er-y-um, I guess so," Stevie says.

"And do you, Maria, promise to be faithful to your husband,
Sam, in sickness and in health, in richer and in poorer, and in
any other type situation?"

"I do!" shouts Mary, with the tone of one who has made it at
last.

John says, "I now pronounce you man and wife." The service
is ended. John says, in the direction of the principals, "You may
kiss the bride."

Stevie takes over, too enthusiastically. Mary, pulling the bride more or less out from under, says, "Sam! Please! We're in public!" John goes to the piano and plays a few bars of the funeral march as a concluding recessional. A mild brawl breaks out. The guests all yell, "The cake! The cake!" Mary says, "Wait, she has to throw her garter belt!"

It is too much for me. "No, no, honey, her garter," I say.

The cake is carefully cut, the pre-engineered plan adhered to with the slight deviation of needing an extra piece for Peter's friend. We even take a picture. Tom says, "I'm embarrassed. Mmmm," as he tastes the cake and wolfs down his piece. Mary and her friends go back to playing dolls, the rest of us go back to reading or the road-race set in the basement. John's troll "minister," his blue hair unwound, returns to his place on the bureau. The wedding is over.

This is not all. They act out heart attacks they hear about, clutching their chests and falling to the floor. Mary, who has had several occasions of being in the hospital, ascribes to hospital patients she hears about experiences more lurid than any she has had, and the others join in. They plan the demise of ministers of Methodist churches in communities where they think they might like to live.

I wonder sometimes whether our touch is too light, whether about some of these matters we should not insist more on the trappings of piety so they will know what is holy to us. I ask my husband about it and he says, "They have such an *accurate* sense of what matters to us." And I'm sure they do, as all children do of their parents.

They have their own moments of holy ground, expressed in their own way, and when I am a spectator to these moments I am grateful. I see Stevie find his pet guinea pig, which has been lost for an hour, and he sits on the ground and strokes it and talks to it, with tears in his eyes. I see the older children filling out cards in church, to join with us in willing their eyes to the Eye Bank. I overhear Mary having articulate religious conversations with her Catholic friends, exchanging points of view, explaining what I have said when at bedtime the night before she asked me what "we believe about baptism." I remember them as very young children coming for the first time to what death is, and as affronted at that scandalous reality as any other human being when this discovery comes to him for the first time. I am moved when Peter, on the first day of ninth grade, finds that the price of school lunch has gone up over the summer and, knowing that neither he nor John, for whom this is the first day of junior high school, will have enough money for a lunch ticket, finds John in the lunch line and gives him his own money "because I thought he needed it worse." I share John's pleasure and quiet pride when, after what has been for him a hard adjustment to the demands of a big, noisy, and confusing junior high, I come home from school Open House and report that two of his teachers have said to me, "I wish I had all students like John."

I am impressed when Peter doesn't want me to point out mistakes he made in his homework "because that would be cheating," or uses particular care in choosing a gift card at Christmastime for his Jewish Den Mother. Or when John, with a little impatience and a perspective I wish some adults had, says, as the other children fuss over who gets to sit by the left window in the back seat, "What difference does it make? I don't care *where* I sit." Or when Stevie insists on giving his spending money, not his saving money, for the school Red Cross drive, or urges his father and me to take some more of his candy, or gives his beloved hand puppet to the children of a family he doesn't know who have lost everything in a fire. I am touched when I come down to get the breakfast one summer morning and find on the kitchen counter a nosegay of purple phlox with a note from Mary, printed in pencil on a torn scrap of paper, "For you, Mom."

So, what matters most to us comes to be included in the stuff of life for them, too. Does it *all* matter to them? Certainly not all of it, though I think they would not violate what is most holy to us, as I think we would not violate what is most holy to them. They do not joke about real sorrow to anyone they know, and the sight of tiny babies at baptism is a moment of uncommon sweetness. They know what love is, because they are daily enmeshed in its web and, we hope, released to its freedom. They know we are believers, because that is the burden of their father's life, and there are ways in which words cannot touch either to demean or to exalt the effect of a father's vocation. They know we are not perfect, though, especially when they are younger, they would defend us outrageously. ("I *know* it wasn't your fault. You didn't see the light was red. Maybe there was a tree in the way.")

We enjoy our children; they are good company. And as we think of their light touch on some of the common ventures of life, we remember the words of a wise man who said, "A man must not be very sure of his God if he cannot laugh in His presence."

IV

I Learn to Speak Methodist

I am a Methodist. It was not always so. I grew up in a Baptist church, and until I went to college I didn't know how little status accrued to being a Baptist, though in the New England city in which I lived the Congregationalists did have the most impressive building and the most prestigious prayer group. When in the course of some early college pleasantries I disclosed to a New Jersey Presbyterian friend that I was a Baptist, she looked at me as one might look at an aborigine who read Homer in the original and said, "How interesting." Indeed. She is still my friend, one of the best. She has become a Unitarian, which far outdoes my slight cultural rise in becoming a Methodist. But I married a Methodist minister, and I am a Methodist.

To a person not used to the language of the Methodist Church it seems strange indeed. Fortunately my husband and I were married while he was in seminary, so I had several years in which to try and get on to the terms before they became such a part of our vocational conversation.

Take the word "conference." Never again will it mean an informal or programed gathering for the consideration of a particular problem. To a Methodist, Conference is always capitalized. But there are many kinds of capitalized Conference—together they define The System—and an understanding of the meanings of this word is as basic to understanding the workings of the Methodist Church as a knowledge of anatomy is to a medical student.

For a novice the most stunning confusion *re* this word Conference probably surrounds the institution called Fourth Quarterly Conference. Contrary to what you might suppose, Fourth Quarterly Conference is not the fourth in a series of quarterly meetings. It is the annual business meeting of a local church, held in the spring, and it is conducted by an administrative superior known as a "D.S." At this meeting church officers are elected, some budgetary items are voted upon, reports of the year's work are given, and plans for the future are discussed.

The interest generated in Fourth Quarterly Conference is in inverse proportion to the state of harmony of the church. If attendance is slight and the meeting is unimpassioned, things are probably going well. But if there is a rousing crowd, with gleams in the eye, the stage is set for action. The presiding officer may try to calm things down by a "spiritual" devotional period preceding the business, but he will shame no one; he might as well save his breath. I have been at a Fourth Quarterly Conference where a member of the Official Board challenged another member to settle their differences outside. Fortunately reason, in the person of an anxious wife, prevailed and the flailing remained verbal. But on and on the public and private oratory flowed, and even the speeches made to "second the motion" kept the proceedings at a purple hum.

Controversy at Fourth Quarterly Conference may focus around

many issues. A favorite is whether or not to expand the educational building or to buy an adjoining property for future use. Whether or not to relocate the church parsonage promises certain disagreement. (The lady who lives in the town mansion will point out that some of our members don't begin to live in as nice houses as the parsonage we have *now*.) Whether to hire a new custodian is also a good hair-raiser, should the excitement lag. The custodian is usually underpaid, and people who have trouble keeping their kitchen floors clean can't see any reason why those scuff marks weren't off the recreation room floor the day after the mother-daughter banquet. A still better leverage against the custodian is the state of the toilets or the disposition of the garbage left in the kitchen after church suppers.

But for high-level drama, for a real Moment of Truth, there is no controversy which can so liven up a Fourth Quarterly Conference as the question: Do You Want Your Minister Back Next Year? (Anyone contemplating the ministry should envision himself in this part of the arena before he makes his final decision. Presumably he is a sensitive fellow or he wouldn't want to be a minister in the first place.) In fact the question, Do You Want Your Minister Back Next Year? is recognized by church authorities to be such a keg of dynamite that it is no longer included in the questions to be dealt with by each Fourth Quarterly Conference.

But there are ways—oh, yes, there are ways. The best way is in the agreed-upon minimum salary for next year. Say the minister has been receiving a salary of $7,000, plus the payment by the church of the utilities expenses for the parsonage. If the budget for the next year suggests a salary of $5,500 and *no* utilities, the minister—who has had four years of college and at least three of seminary—will know all is not well. In fact, he will have known it before. For prior to the day of a really hot Fourth Quarterly Conference the minister's phone will have been jumping, his doorstep never empty, his office a rallying point for all members of his side of the controversy, who are bringing the latest strategy plans, the last word from the underground, as to what "they" plan to do at the meeting and what "we" are going to do to keep the initiative.

For there is no loyalty more profound and no antagonism more unyielding than those which swirl around the head of a servant of the Lord when the members of a congregation divide on that great issue of Methodism's annual springtime frontier: Do You Want Your Minister Back Next Year? and a minister who goes through his career without being at the eye of such a hurricane just does not know what he is missing. Our family lore would be much poorer if, in moments of crisis, we could not remind each other of that man who rose to his feet to "second the motion" in a five-minute speech of flaming words and waving arms, or of his married son who at a quieter moment said to my husband, "Some of us are so loyal to you that if you announced a marble-shooting contest in the church parking lot, we'd be there." It's enough to make a convert out of anyone.

I suppose I should say a word about the calm waters of a more ordinary Fourth Quarterly Conference. For they do predominate, though they are nowhere near as interesting. The reports are duly given, the salary decided, the minister knows his services for next year are urgently desired, many pleasantries are exchanged, the presiding officer enriches the group with his devotional remarks and his encouragement, and, at the refreshments provided after the meeting by the Woman's Society of Christian Service, not a hand or a coffee cup trembles. But as for those others—to quote the quote of a favorite Bishop, "The church must be divine. Otherwise it would never have lasted so long."

So much for the Fourth Quarterly Conference, which is not the fourth and which comes once a year. There is another annual meeting which bears some, though not much, relation to Fourth Quarterly Conference, and it is called First Quarterly Conference. It is held in the fall, often on a Sunday afternoon, and it is always at some other far-off church. At First Quarterly Conference representatives of several churches meet together to consider matters that are supposed to be of joint interest. Information and inspiration about the coming year's program are given out in unwieldy doses. Both those who are bugged on church meetings and go anyway and those who because of some office they hold in the local church cannot avoid going attend in sleepy numbers and usually get little inspiration and entirely too much information.

At First Quarterly Conference there is also opportunity given for a particular local church to decide on any important matters that cannot wait the many months until its Fourth Quarterly Conference. This is a splendid chance for pulling off some sneaky decisions, since the home guard, not realizing something important is up, will stay home with the Sunday paper, and "we" can casually have our decisions passed and recorded while "they," who were eligible to attend but did not, have no one but themselves to sputter at.

As for Second and Third Quarterly Conferences, try to find them. I have been the wife of a Methodist minister for over twelve years and I've yet to hear of one.

Next in line of ascending size is the District Conference. The District Conference is an annual one-day affair, at which pastors and lay representatives of the fifty to one hundred or so churches comprising a District tend to those housekeeping duties that have a broader base of operation than the local church unit. (Since the District Conference is usually held on a business day, say from 9:30 A.M. to 3:30 P.M., the aggregate of lay representatives looks like a mix of Ladies' Day and Golden Age Club.) At the District Conference licenses to preach are granted to beginning clergymen and supply pastors. The churches are informed of the coming presence in the District of a missionary on furlough, and they are urged to "sign him up" for meetings with the women, the church school, a family night supper. There is the ubiquitous batch of "inspirational talks": efforts by various program leaders to jack up the enthusiasm of the group for whichever interest—education, evangelism, missions—that leader represents. While District Conference does have important tasks (particularly the granting of licenses to preach), in many minds it seems to get lost in the shuffle—and there is certainly plenty of shuffle to get lost in.

There remain four other meanings of this Methodist word Conference. The first is a Conference as a geographical administrative unit. It is headed by a Bishop, who is probably head of one or two other Conferences, and these comprise the Bishop's Area. To be elected a Bishop is a great honor, and once a man has been so elected he will need the honor to sustain him, as "criticize the Bishop" is one of the favorite back-room games of almost everyone else sufficiently involved in the Church to know that Bishop is not always a chess piece.

Between the office of Bishop and the scattered workings of the ministers stands, in the Methodist Conference (as a geographical

administrative unit), the marvelous institution of the "D.S." Now
D.S. does not mean Department of Sanitation, though there are
certain analogous features which we oughtn't to press too far.
D.S. means District Superintendent, and the D.S., as he is always
referred to, is the administrative middleman between the Bishop
of the Conference and the Men. A D.S. is appointed by the
Bishop from the upper ranks of the ministers, and to these ranks,
either during or at the end of his six-year term, he will return,
though at a level in keeping with his now greater status as an
"ex-D.S."

A D.S. may have fifty to a hundred ministers in his care, and
his functions as their caretaker are several. He is supposed to
keep his men in line with the general aims and programs of the
Church, so that if this is the year to Search Our Hearts, or Win
America for Christ, the D.S. sees to it that the men busy themselves with Searching or Winning. For this purpose he will relay
to them many forms, papers, brochures, and report blanks on
which they are to record the intensity and extent of their Search-
ings and Winnings. He may also institute some system of checks
and balances where the ministers visit back and forth in each
other's parishes. The professed aim of this cross-fertilization is
to infuse each local congregation with the fresh inspiration of a
new personality. A crasser function of this back-and-forth visita-
tion is to see that no one goofs off on the job of Searching or
Winning: after all, if an administrative proxy is coming to aug-
ment your efforts, you're pretty sure to have some efforts to aug-
ment.

This reciprocal visiting is looked upon somewhat dimly by
many of the ministers. It is viewed even more dimly by the min-

isters' wives as, during the week when "he" is visiting "us," chances are we get to feed and house him, and while he may be a delightful guest, still the children have to be on company behavior, the meals (including breakfast!) have to be company meals, and the week stretches on. Worse yet for the wife of the minister is the other in this pair of weeks, when her husband blesses the distant congregation—and parsonage—with his presence; she sees too little of her husband as it is, and while for the first day or two she may enjoy the ease of feeding the family cereal and peanut butter sandwiches three meals a day, she soon finds herself vacuously saying to the children every two hours, "I wonder what Daddy's doing now."

In addition to his supervisory role in carrying out the church's program, the D.S. is supposed to be available as a counselor to his men. The unfeasibility of this procedure is soon evident, as a man's future career may depend on his D.S.'s report that he is wholly adequate in all situations. Who would go to the determiner of his promotions and say, "Dr. Wilson, I am lousy at youth work," or, "I am having an affair with the choir director and I don't know how to break it off"? This is hardly likely to bring about a move to wider fields of service.

It is in the matter of moves, of appointments to churches, that the D.S. exerts some of his greatest influence over the ministers in his care. The several D.S.'s and the Bishop of a Conference make up the Cabinet for that Conference, and a chief job of the Cabinet is to match the maybe six hundred men with six hundred churches. Happily, they don't all upheave at once. Some years are considered a good year to move, and there is a lot of fluidity and many new appointments are made. Some years are considered bad years to move; choices are limited and only "the problem children" are moved—probably traded around with, it is hoped, the minimum disastrous effect among a possibly equal number of "problem churches."

During such a year no one moves who doesn't have to. Who wants to be known as a problem child if, by sticking it out for one more year, he can move in the company of the blessed— those many ministers who, in a good year, move for the benefit of themselves, for the benefit of the churches which after poignant testimonial farewells they have just left, for the benefit of the larger churches into which they are joyously received, or even, perhaps, for the benefit of the faith? To be in on this awesome responsibility of deciding the moves is one of the chief jobs of a D.S., and there is not a minister who passes by his D.S. in the light of day or the dark of night who can completely free himself from the radar-communicated message: He may have something to say about where I go next. Nor is there a D.S. who, try as he may to put his men at ease and be "one of the boys," can free himself from the onus and privilege of being a Supervisor.

For this as for other reasons being a D.S. is considered, at least in open conversation, to be an unenviable position. Who wants to have to conduct all those Fourth Quarterly Conferences, referee all those local fights, and send out, receive back, and send on to the Bishop all those forms and reports? Who wants to have to breathe down the neck of seventy-five individualistic ministers, each of whom would probably like to be left alone to carry on his ministry as *he* sees fit? Besides, a D.S. has no local congregation of which he is the harried shepherd—no one to think of him as Mr. Wonderful (or even as Mr. Awful, since some kind of attention is better than none).

Becoming a D.S. is sometimes referred to as "going on the District," something like "going on the rock pile" or another form of imprisoning activity. One D.S., in looking forward to the end of his six-year term "on the District," used to say, "Now when I get back into Christian work. . . ." However, to be a D.S. has Decided Status and some power, and most men who have been offered the job have not turned it down. Besides, if a D.S. can stick it out for his six-year term—or less, if duty calls him elsewhere—he is in an unusually apt position for helping return himself to the pastorate at a congenial spot. For as the end of his term approaches, he sits in deferential and suggestive silence, in good rapport with the rest of the Cabinet, as the choice vacancies of the Conference are placed upon the table for action.

So much, then, for Conference as a geographical administrative unit and for the method of administering it. Let us move on to another meaning: Annual Conference. Annual Conference is to Methodists at once a political party convention, an audience with the Pope, a glorified gossip session, a holy gathering, a four-day night on the town, and a family reunion. As Fourth Quarterly Conference is to a local church, so Annual Conference is to the Conference-as-a-geographical-administrative-unit just described.*

Annual Conference is usually held in the late spring or early summer, to correspond with the end of the school year. This is because the moves of pastors (and their families) to different churches, which are made known at Annual Conference, become effective immediately. If the minister and his family cannot complete their link in the chain of moves by next Sunday, at least the

---

* Actually, this is a slight oversimplification. The legal name of Conference-as-a-geographical-administrative-unit is also Annual Conference. But it is almost never referred to as such, and I have left it off here.

husband will be at his new pulpit, being scrutinized by the members of his new congregation.

He will usually have a large attendance out on his first Sunday, and if he wants to read from the *Bhagavad Gita,* he may, because his person and mannerisms will be under such careful observation his words will scarcely be noticed. If he can delay bringing his wife and family until the second Sunday, he will have a good attendance then, too, as they are only slightly less interesting to behold than he is. After the viewings are completed, the attendance will probably fall off. The minister should not be discouraged: it is nothing personal, and he will see these people again at Christmastime.

At Annual Conference all kinds of business matters are attended to. The Committees give their reports. The champion of Temperance makes his customary plea for greater emphasis on total abstinence from alcoholic beverages, after which the Committee on Schools and Colleges reports its recommendation that our support of Methodist-related colleges in no way be contingent on forbidding the students to have alcohol in their rooms. The Committee on Evangelism urges the appointment of a full-time Secretary of Evangelism, and the Board of Education reports that its needs for additional personnel should have top priority if the Conference can afford another staff person—in fact, the whole educational program of the church is in immediate jeopardy if another Secretary cannot be hired. The Commission on Worship reports on the new hymnal and the workshops on worship held during the past year and suggests meaningful participation in worship as the basis for the Christian life. The Commission on Social Concerns, for some of whose members the careful study of worship seems a preoccupation with irrelevant voodoo, urges the Conference's endorsement of fair housing practices and the right to demonstrate and its opposition to harness racing and state lotteries. The Missions Commission reports on mission work in the United States and abroad, the Conference Historical Society enthusiastically reports on its esoteric activities, and the Conference Pension Plan is described in worldly detail.

There is usually at least one merger—of two Conferences, of two denominations, or of previously autonomous racial groups —under consideration at every session of Annual Conference. This subject, whatever form it takes this year, is good for several bottles of blood-pressure medicine. There are always pros and cons from the supporters of each, some Monday morning quarterbacking about the success or failure of previous mergers, some propheteering about what this merger may lead to, and appeals to conscience, practicality, and the will of God. Take a hundred ministers each with strong feeling on the subject and at least half of the hundred eager to express his feelings, and you have as many words and much more passion than at a Senate filibuster. (There are lay delegates to Annual Conference, too, usually one per church, but they are not as voluble as the ministers, who feel the real show of Annual Conference belongs to them.)

Over this many-faceted orgy of organized confusion presides the Bishop, and it is here that his most sterling qualities are called into play. The items of the agenda must all be dealt with, yet the Bishop doesn't want unnecessarily to squelch debate. Since many of those who "speak to the motion" are willing for a side effect to impress the Bishop, he is aware of himself as an audience of one to a six-hundred-member cast. He does have the interest of the Church at heart and would like to get on with the business in as harmonious a manner as possible. If he has a sense of humor, now is the time to bring it out. It will cushion his impatience when some perennial "hair shirt in residence" rises to make his annual twenty-minute speech protesting the violation of our treaty with the Indians or the dropping of a favorite hymn from the 1935 edition of the hymnal, and it will help him clear the air when the debate on any one of a dozen issues has been over all available ground three times and is about to start on the fourth time around.

In our Conference the sessions begin with the singing of an old Wesley hymn, starting, "And are we yet alive?" It is not a rhetorical question, and the assembled men, mentally leaping around in some of the high and low spots of their last year's work, may have some wry and ironic thoughts about the viability of their professional life.

On the last day, the Annual Conference, after passing memorials of thanks to all the cooks, janitors, and chairmen of housing for carrying out arrangements for its comfort and care, and to the local police department for providing meter-free parking, concludes its sessions with the climactic ordination of the new ministers and the reading of the appointments for next year. There is always a huge crowd, and no one inquires too carefully whether the crowd is there to participate in the holy service of ordination or to get the final authoritative word on the rumors flying around during Conference—and for many moons previous —about who is going where. The Big Appointments are common knowledge by now, but the news about moves among the lower echelons is almost as interesting and much less threatening than the stunner about the man ten years out of seminary who is going to the seventh largest church in the Conference, and at a $1,500 raise in salary.

The last day of Conference is always a hot day, the church is never air-conditioned, and the program is usually behind schedule. Nevertheless, the end is in sight; the suitcases are packed and in the car. The urge for speed is present. The words of ordination have to be repeated at each occasion of the Bishop's "laying on of hands," and they are intoned with all reverent speed. One Bishop cut the time of this part of the service in half by ordaining two men at a time, putting his left hand on the head of one and his right hand on the head of the next one—a practice which caused a member of the ordination committee who was a stickler for purer liturgics to mutter to a fellow clergyman beside him, "Too bad the Bishop ain't an octopus!"

After the Ordination Service the Bishop reads the appointments, the Superindent of each District standing by the Bishop as the appointments to that District are read. This reading is done in as close to a monotone as possible—a kind of neo-Greek device to heighten, à la the masks, the drama of the event. After the reading, Annual Conference is adjourned and the men leave for home, mulling over the appointments, the resolutions, the convolutions of the actions taken, their own feelings about being ministers, and the sure prospect of being met at the door of home by the scintillating question, "Well, how was Conference?"

There is still, among the various meanings of the word Conference, the institution of General Conference, which is the world gathering of the Methodist Church that meets once every four years. General Conference is of heroic proportions; there is nothing folksy about it. It meets in a big civic center; banners welcoming it hang from hotel marquees; its actions are reported world-wide. It is the outward and visible sign of Methodism gone big-time. To be elected by your Annual Conference as one of its three or four ministerial or lay delegates is a great honor. For a layman it is a recognition of church statesmanship; for a minister, it will do in lieu of being made a Bishop. To the thousands of observers who come to attend its open sessions, General Conference is complex, maddening, and occasionally inspiring. To its delegates it is an assigned seat and a vote, a lot of study papers and extra meetings, perhaps a chance to speak, and . . . complex, maddening, and occasionally inspiring. It is the machinery at work, trying to keep the Church relevant. To a Methodist who among the large institutions of society feels insecure of his "place," it should be reassuring.

There is one more. Between the institutions of Annual Conference and General Conference stands, in the United States, the awkward stepchild, Jurisdictional Conference. It, too, meets every four years, is a regional enclave, and its chief function is to fill any vacancies among the Bishops. If there happen to be no vacancies to fill that year, the Jurisdictional Conference assembles for its three days anyway, fraternally whoops it up, and probably hears a succession of speeches on how the Jurisdictional System is now outmoded and should be done away with.

It is interesting to note that the foregoing causes for confusion in Methodist terminology are related to the polity and government of the Church rather than to such intricacies as Presbyterian theology or Baptist preoccupations with freedom and individuality. Not, we charitably assume, that Methodists don't care about theology and freedom. But as a party platform it is a little less dangerous to be significantly wrong about Conference Apportionments than about Predestination or Eternal Security.

A final irony now rears its ecumenical head. Having at last and to my private satisfaction pulled some Methodist order out of the myriad uses of that once simple word "conference," I must realign the whole thing. For on April 23, 1968, and after many years of small group conversations, discussions, committee gatherings, and reports, and after untold hours of general discussions on the floors of First Quarterly Conferences, Fourth Quarterly Conferences, District Conferences, Annual Conferences, Jurisdictional Conferences, and yea, verily, General Conferences, the Methodist Church and the Evangelical United Brethren Church (known in the trade as "the E.U.B.'s") merged to become the United Methodist Church. The new uses of the word "conference" are a compromise between Methodist and "E.U.B." uses— at least our traditions have used the same word.

I am told the changes actually simplify this "conference" fugue. I am told that the main difference for ex-Methodists is that First Quarterly Conference is dropped and that Fourth Quarterly Conference is now known as "the Charge Conference." I am told that this has nothing to do with deferred payment, but that it refers to the assembled Official Boards of the church or churches under the leadership of one pastor. I am told that should the Official Board of one of the churches under the leadership of a pastor want to meet without the Official Board or Boards of the other church or churches also under the leadership of that pastor, the resulting gathering is known as a church Local Conference. Or that if, on the other hand, the combined Official Boards of a charge see fit to invite the whole congregation to the annual meeting, that gathering shall be known as the Annual Congregational Meeting. But that if, in a mood of camaraderie, the churches under the leadership of two or more pastors want to meet *together, that* gathering is a Joint Charge Conference. See how simple it is? It is enough to make even the most stalwart throw up his United Methodist hands, shake his United Methodist head, and wonder: If a Joint Charge Annual Congregational Meeting comes, then, out of self-defense if not Christian love, can consolidation be far behind?

V

Pre-Parson Parsonages

To a minister and his family, home is a jerkily changing scene. All houses, either entered or scanned, are potential parsonages, not only to the minister and his wife but to the children as well. Rides through the country take on a house-viewing character, and old grayed barns about to fall will probably bring the comment from one of the family, "That would be a nice parsonage —air-conditioned, even." A minister's wife with a practiced eye can give a good guess at a house's floor plan while driving past at forty miles an hour, and we are perhaps second only to real estate men in our ability to give a quick evaluation of the living qualities of any house we see.

In fact we may outdo real estate men in our feeling for houses. I remember discussing a house we had recently toured as a possible new parsonage with a real estate man who was a member of one of our churches. The house had the prescribed number of rooms, but these were so small as to be constricting not only of furniture but of motion and ease. I suggested that they reminded me of Frank Lloyd Wright's description of a type of house as being "a prison for the human spirit." The man looked startled and let it pass.

It is not only that we have lived in a good many houses, most of us; we have been in many others, as we have visited our ministerial friends, and we have seen still others as we have evaluated a potential "call" partly in terms of how our family might fit into the living space that goes with it. (This last consideration is viewed with disdain by many ministers, who feel that the house that goes with a "call" is a materialistic consideration and should have nothing to do with whether or not the minister goes to a particular place. I am not of this mind, though I have enough misgivings on the subject not to be too noisy in the good discussion you can get going in almost any ministers' wives' group by waving this particular red flag.)

To me, who grew up remembering only one home, who was married from the house our family moved into on my second birthday, where my parents still live, a succession of homes that were not my own stretched ahead of me an as adventure of dubious desirability. "Home" to me was a white house with an apple tree and lilies of the valley on the north side, a living room that opened onto a south porch, and a hill for winter sliding. But such a stationary image of home was not to be ours. We have lived, during the nearly seventeen years of our marriage, in nine dwellings, and through this succession of student and pastoral houses and apartments I feel I am such a connoisseur of dwelling places —of what works best and what is nice but unnecessary—that almost I am old before my time as far as knowledgeable appraisal of houses goes.

Before my husband and I were married, which was during his first year of seminary, the question came up as to whether he should take as his seminary field work an assistantship in a church which would offer, as part of its payment to him, the use of part of its parsonage. So the long succession of speculation about parsonages began. We would not be the only occupants of the house. There were two other ministerial students living there, too, in various stages of domesticity. One of the men was married, and he and his wife had a small baby. The other student was a bachelor, and these men, along with my husband, would form the group ministry of the church across the street, in a neighborhood which was old, pleasant, and had seen better days. Into this ménage my brand-new husband and I would move—if he wished to take the job.

He described the house to me. It was big: it had thirteen rooms and a front and back stairs; the rooms included a collection of parlors and bedrooms and studies and a large pantry off the large kitchen, and one bathroom, which, in addition to opening onto the main upstairs hall, opened onto the room my husband and I would occupy. The house was furnished.

Furthermore, Hoyt had talked at some length with the other two men and the wife of the one who had a wife, and he assured me they were very pleasant and would be most considerate and cooperative; the wife had suggested that I adopt the large pantry as my private domain in the kitchen and she was sure we could happily share the refrigerator, stove, and sink. My husband and I thought we would prefer eating by ourselves, at least at first, to eating community meals, and this arrangement would be fine with the other men and the one already established wife. It was decided that on an appointed day I would make the short train trip from my home city to the seminary town, to meet the present occupants of the house and to pass on this as a possible home for us.

On my way down I tried to envision what the house would be like. My image of furnished Methodist parsonages included everyone's unmatched castoffs and, somewhere in some room of the house, one of those old-time umbrella stands with upper projections, or "antlers," on which to hang hats. Apart from the house, how would I like the other occupants, and living so closely with other people in the first weeks of our marriage?

I arrived at the train station, Hoyt met me, and we took the bus out to the parsonage in question.

My impressions of our evening together are dim. I remember a pleasant candlelit dinner, some conversation in which I got theologically over my head, a sense of present and future compatibility with the other members of the household, a detailed tour through what seemed like endless and inadequately lit rooms —some of them kept closed off to save on heating bills—a huge kitchen with a pleasant windowed pantry, and in the front hall, which evidently was hardly ever used, an old oak stand, with a lift-lid seat for housing boots, an iron-curlicued side arm for supporting umbrellas, a high mirror forming the back of this "chair," and on top of the mirror and branching out into the room a magnificent arrangement of "antlers" on which to hang your hat. Hoyt took the job and, in due time, we moved in.

The six months we spent in that parsonage were a combination of pleasure, hilarity, and some distress. I would not recommend to any couple that they start out marriage in as unprivate an arrangement as this. As any counselor will tell you, there is enough adjustment in getting used to one another without adding complications, no matter how considerate and well-meaning the complications may be. The church took a kind of romantic interest in us as a newly married pair, as did the young bachelor in the house, who used to perform his late-evening ablutions in the bathroom outside our bedroom door while humming "Good night, Irene" in loud tones. He also cautioned us against embracing in the dining room lest anyone looking in through one of the room's many windows should see us, so we used to wait until we knew he was going by outside and then fall into each other's arms. He used to talk to me about how distressed he was with the occasional clutter of family equipment left around by Jane, the other wife in the household—a distress with which I was sympathetic until I glimpsed one day the complete havoc of the interior of the room which was his.

The two upstairs rooms that were ours were at the end of the hall near the bathroom, and their decor was a little grim. One of the two was kept unheated and we used it as a guest room, adding to its spare furnishings such suitable wedding presents as would liven its bleakness but which were not sufficiently to our taste to go into our own room. Our room had the necessary furniture, and heat in the radiator, and a hideous brown-and-orange squared linoleum on the floor, which we painted to a more subdued but still shiny brown.

The house was not only community property to the six of us (including the baby) who lived there, but the church people considered it as a social annex to the church and held many meetings in the most-often-used parlor. One evening as we were finishing dinner some of the ladies showed up at the front door, informed us that there was to be a meeting there that evening, and brought their refreshments for the affair into the kitchen, where I was still fixing our dessert. Their use of the house was not usually this impromptu, and when they did appear apparently unannounced it was due to some failure of communication among the five of us adults, one of whom had probably been informed of the coming meeting but forgot to tell the others.

It was in this house that I first encountered the euphemism, "Your minister is as near as your telephone," which the bachelor minister, who was the "titular head" of the parish, had printed in the weekly bulletin. The only telephone the church had was the one in the parsonage, and Jane and I were the receiving service for most casual, business, or emergency calls that came in. While it was in our case true that at least one of the ministers' wives was "as near as your telephone," any parishioner naïve enough to take the bulletin statement literally was usually disappointed.

A very good feature of our nearness to the church was the natural assumption, which Jane and I encouraged, that food left over from church suppers would be put to good use by the several adults who occupied the parsonage, and we used regularly to count on having our dinner the day after a church supper from the leftovers of that affair.

The church ladies included some excellent cooks. There was a pair of maiden sisters whose hobby was cooking and who used what seemed to us budgeting young housewives fantastic amounts of eggs and butter; they often brought us samples of their productions. Our bachelor inhabitant had a tendency to put on weight under this rain of goodies, plus some extra ones he was offered on pastoral calls, particularly by the several ladies who considered him an eligible prospect, but he protested he was virtually powerless to help himself—after all, the ladies offered it to him. To which my husband replied, "That was Adam's excuse," and thereby, in our theological domain, brought down the house.

In June Hoyt's field work changed to working as an aide in the community mental hospital. We moved from our thirteen-room house to be sole occupants of one half a semifurnished quonset hut in a student housing project known as Armoryville, which had been erected after World War II as "emergency housing" and which, six years later, was still going strong. Here, in this three-room inverted semicircle I felt, at last, like a queen in my own castle.

Each housing unit had, extending across its width, a combination room which served as kitchen-dining room on one side and living room on the other. Behind this were a small bathroom with a shower stall (the room was too small for a tub) and two bedrooms. The larger bedroom was big enough for a double bed and two chests of drawers, but you had to stand to one side of the one chest, or else kneel on the bed, to get the drawers open. The small bedroom was used either as a study or as a child's—or children's—bedroom. The units were heated by an unsightly space heater set approximately in the middle of the hut and therefore at the back edge of the living room. These were fed by university-supplied coal, hauled in by the bucketful from wooden bins outside. In summer the huts got so hot students who had hoses ran their spray over the roof during the hottest part of the day. But the huts cooled off at night, and the outdoors was always available if the inside got unbearably hot. There was a story going around that at one time a particularly wealthy student couple had inhabited one of these half-huts while their maid had been housed at the city's best hotel.

The quadrangle had a community laundry building, a maintenance office, clothesline and coalbins between each set of two huts, and pleasant sidewalks along the road that followed its U shape.

At football season, because it was near the university football field and therefore had prime parking space, the quadrangle could be entered only with the passes given out to all residents at the beginning of the year.

The place abounded with children. This particular graduate student housing area was known by the University Hospital Obstetrics Department as "fertile valley." There were students living here with as many as four children, and they managed in such small space with marvelous ingenuity. We went to visit a divinity school couple in one of them who had three children, and their "hut," as we always referred to our dwellings, looked like an ad from a home-furnishings magazine.

In the spirit of the place, we, too, had our first baby while we were living here, losing the race with another divinity school couple who had gone with us through the latter stages of incipient parenthood: their baby arrived a week before Christmas, ours not until December 23. They took their small baby daughter home to their small bedroom, which they had painted a masculine blue; we brought our nine-pound son home to our small bedroom, newly painted pink. The other mother and I joined the group of really "in" quadrangle wives—those with new or very recently arrived babies. Exchanges of maternity clothes (for the next time around) and receiving blankets, appreciative viewings of baby gifts, discussions of the pros and cons of natural childbirth and breast feeding, commiserations over the scarcity of sleep all became the order of the day. We had baby-sitting clubs, with elaborate point systems distinguishing between daytime (babies awake—more points earned) and evening hours (babies asleep—fewer points earned) and less formal arrangements. We conferred on the decorating possibilities of our huts —whether contrasting or harmonizing curtains were more pleasing at the shallow windows, and what could be done to camouflage the kitchen appliances, which, after all, sat at one end of the living room. One fellow student, now a famous theologian and social commentator, whom my husband remembers as a brashly articulate seminary student, lives in my mind as the dinner guest who remarked, when I foolishly asked him how he liked the new curtains I had just made, "Well, o.k., but I prefer something a little brighter myself."

In the quadrangle we did a good bit of entertaining of one another. And in between times someone was always available for counsel or just to chat. We could engage in domestic talk if we wanted, but the wives as well as the husbands usually had education and interest in more far-flung issues as well.

We lived in our Armoryville palace for two happy years. The second year there, which was Hoyt's third and last year of divinity school, he met his field work requirement by serving as a youth worker at a church in a nearby town. This time, however, the arrangement did not call for us to live in the church parsonage, and I, with a new baby to care for, preserved an uninvolved and mutually acceptable distance from the church itself, though I did enjoy the young people, when I included myself in their activities or on the several occasions when one or all of them came to our hut to visit.

At the end of two years, after Hoyt's graduation from divinity school, we sold such furnishings as we would not need, bought a few others—all on the flea market of the Armoryville exchange

—and moved to what would be our last non-church-affiliated dwelling, three and a half rooms on the sixth and top floor of a handsome brick garden apartment building in the Riverdale section of the Bronx in New York City, where Hoyt was going to pursue one year's further graduate study.

The spiritual isolation in the midst of physical crowding is legendary in New York, and for the first few weeks after my husband would go off to his work in the morning the day would stretch ahead of me long and lonely, with only my infant son for company. I came to understand—as I never again had the occasion to, as a parsonage wife—how lonely you can feel when you move as a stranger into a new city and have to carve out a "place" for yourself.

Before long I met and became good friends with two other young women, each with a small baby, and we would stroll our babies together in the park or chat in the basement laundry. One of the young women and her husband had a television set, and she invited the rest of us to some of the more sensational episodes of the Army-McCarthy hearings and, in the evenings, to share in some of the concerts that were available on the television networks. Our three husbands were all involved in graduate work of one kind or another, and the six of us formed a community within the community of the apartment house.

The isolation of the city became more legendary than real: strolls in the park brought encounters with other young mothers, including one pleasant young woman whose name was Hebe and whose tiny son bore the given names of Francis Xavier, though his mother always referred to him as "X." Meetings in the hallway, at the mailboxes, on the elevator soon extended our speaking acquaintance to many of the apartment families.

With the family in the apartment beneath us, our acquaintance was maintained on rather strained terms. Our sympathy was all with the family, but we didn't know what to do. Our small son was an energetic child, and upon awaking, either in the morning, the late evening, or the middle of the night, was in the habit of rising on all fours and rocking his bed back and forth with enough vigor that it staccatoed around the room, making, I am sure, a truly tremendous racket over the heads of the people below us. They called us several times, on these occasions, urging us to come down and listen. Were we sanding the floor at 2:30 A.M.? Did we have a herd of elephants up there? We assured them of our sympathy, but we didn't know what to do. There was no way to tie the crib in place. We really could not afford to cover the floor with carpeting. We tried several kinds of rubberized cups under the four casters of the crib. We tried removing the casters, but the noise was even worse and the floor was in danger of being badly scratched. The child was not unhappy; he was not desirous of getting up: he was, evidently, getting some extra nocturnal exercise.

These unfortunate occupants of the apartment below were known to us by telephone only until one day when, coming down in the elevator, a pleasant-looking woman who got on at the fifth floor said to me, in an all-too-familiar voice, "Is this"—nodding toward my son, sitting in docile silence in his stroller—"the young man who rides around in his bed?" I admitted that he was indeed the culprit, we recognized each other as persons of humane intention, and with some generously benevolent clucking on her part the conversation ended.

The apartment house was, in its own limited terms, a melting pot. The other graduate student couples we knew had come from

California and England. Some of the occupants had regular maids, and others of us sent our husbands' shirts to the laundry as a special indulgence of ourselves. Another woman, who lived on our floor with her two teen-age daughters, used pathetically to try to convince me that this was the happiest time of my life and that she wished her children were young again. The family that lived on the other side of us was a volatile group: the walls of the apartments were not sufficiently thick to keep us from hearing many of the loud arguments with which they seemed to pepper their lives. A family across the courtyard, in a different building from us, was known to us by the recognizable shadows that passed back and forth in front of the always-drawn shades that faced toward the table where we ate.

June came and, the graduate degree being acquired, we moved again, this time to the very different world of our own church parsonage, the first—with the exception of our brief stay in the community parsonage in New Haven—in a succession of houses not of our choosing, houses that went with churches, houses that were for the most part middle-aged and homey, houses that have been home to us and yet about which it was never quite possible to feel, Now, this is really my home.

VI
Parsonages Proper

A church parsonage absorbs into its walls through the years of its occupancy some memory of the people who have lived in it, and there exists, also, a kind of vertical fellowship among the families that have called that house their home.

Even if the present occupants of the house do not know the people who have lived there before, they come to feel acquainted with them as with, at least, some distant and legendary cousin. The history of the house divides into the periods of occupancy of the pastors' families that lived there, and the church people will describe the placement of furniture, the allocation of rooms, the acquisition of some drapes, or the covering of a wall under previous occupants—"We took that archway out when the Knights were here," or "Mrs. Adams chose that red and white wallpaper in the hall," or "The Philathea Class remodeled the kitchen when Allports lived in the house." So there grows a bond between all the people, known and unknown, who have inhabited a parsonage, and the grown children of parsonage families, re-living their nomad years, may come back at any time to a parsonage that has been home to them and be greeted by its present occupants as returning members of the family.

Church parsonages are, for the most part, sturdy dwellings, and they last a long time. They house families for which they are (so I am told!) too large, and families for which they are too small, and there is much to be said for the alternate custom of not having a church parsonage at all but of including in the minister's salary something commensurate to a housing allowance, so that a family chooses its own dwelling, appropriate to its size and taste. But if you are not going to settle in a community "for good" there is much to be said, too, for having the house there, ready, accessible, a convenient distance from the church (though, it is hoped, not right next door) so one does not have to add the confusions of house hunting to the other burdens of moving. There is, in a life punctuated by moves, a certain continuity, too, in living in "the house that goes with the church," so that even though your own family's tenure may be no more than several years, the house extends its shelter in either direction —before you and after you—and maybe, as you live in the house, you take on by osmosis some of the security of a longer stay by living in this, the church's "home."

If you are present, as we have been, as the first occupants of a house newly acquired as a church parsonage, you will feel a particular investment of yourselves as the first minister's family to live in the house, to "season" it for what you hope will be long years of use. And if you are present, as we have been, at the end of a line, as the last occupants of a house that is due to be torn down, you will be enriched by the meaning of that moment, too. As walls fall away, as inner recesses of closets and bedrooms and halls are exposed to the unaccustomed gaze of the whole world, as floors are undermined and crumble into the wide pit of the basement, what ghosts of previous dwellers will stand around commenting to one another as this shared home of them all returns in rubble to the earth? What echoes of "the Lord's song in a strange land"—sometimes shouted, whispered, or neglected, in triumph or in sorrow—are heard to mix with the sifting fall of dust as the house goes down?

As a parsonage stands as reminder of a bond among the many families who have lived in it, so does the life of a minister's family form in that family's collective memory against a succession of background sceneries, the parsonages it has lived in. Our first parsonage—the home to which we came after Hoyt had received his extra graduate degree and been given this, his first pastoral appointment—was a cream-colored frame dwelling set in a row of houses on a tree-lined street on the upper slopes of a small Pennsylvania town. The town was built around the operation of a chain of coal mines but, unlike some mining communities, this was a town of considerable resource and variety, because the company district headquarters was located here. The Methodist church, I suppose in ironic keeping with its stance in the community, was part way up the hill between the town's main street, along and below which most of the blue-collar workers lived, and the spacious hilltop home of the state senator, who was also the community's most affluent car dealer. The parsonage was a half block away from the church. It had a front porch that stretched across the width of the house, and coming as we did from a high brick apartment house in New York City the luxury and openness of a porch were a special welcome. The center door of the house opened onto a lovely entrance hall, many times larger than the "dining area" foyer which had been our master bedroom in the apartment. As I stood in that hallway for the first time, sensing the meaning of this first parsonage and first pastorate in what would be a long succession of moves and homes and communities in this lifework on which Hoyt was now embarking, I felt some of the tensions—about leaving the environs of my loved New England, about how I was going to manage without the security of a home of our own—felt some of this fall away, at least to the outer walls of this lovely house which already gave us a spacious refuge. This building, while it was not really ours and would not house us for more than several years, already felt like home—a place for us and our children, a place with room enough to move freely, a place with earth close beneath it and earth and air around it and a slow and gentle street outside its door. I turned to my husband as he waited—anxious, I knew, about how I, facing this new way of life with trepidation and very soon to give birth to our second child, was going to take to this place—and said, "Oh, it's lovely. I like it very much," and together we moved inside.

On one side of the hallway was a study and on the other side the living room. Behind the hallway was the dining room and through the dining room you walked to a back hall, then to a pantry and a large kitchen. Upstairs were four bedrooms and a bath, and above that an attic.

Some of the floors of the house were startling. The three rooms in front were carpeted in a deep rose carpeting—very nice. The smallest bedroom, which we planned to use as a nursery for the new baby, had linoleum on the floor—fine. The wood floor of another bedroom, which would be Peter's, was stained with a striated varnish. But three other rooms had floors finished with a varnished strip around the outside of the room and a large square of unfinished raw wood in the middle. We surmised that rugs were supposed to be put down to cover the raw wood. We had one rug only, which left two rooms to go. We had no great surplus of capital, so we got a pair of straw veranda rugs—we told ourselves they gave the place a modern Oriental flavor—and distributed our furniture, supplemented by generous additions from each of our families. We bought a few curtains for the upstairs windows, hung our pictures, and got nicely settled in the two weeks before our second son, John, made his slightly early arrival on the scene.

The front hallways of homes are important, not only for their symbolic importance as passageways between the inside and outside worlds but because memorable events do seem to happen there. The front hallway of our first parsonage, with its green pine-coned wallpaper and deep rose rug, lives in my mind as the place where, soon after our move, Peter, just a year and a half, on seeing that we had moved the door hook from a height where he could reach it to the eye level of adults, nodded to himself and muttered, "I get the stickyard," and, a master mechanic even then, toddled off to find the yardstick he had in mind and, returning, juggle it under the high hook until once again he had released the hook from its metal eye and himself—had he not been stopped—to wander at will outside. I see Peter again in the front hall, perhaps a year older by now, greeting a bachelor minister friend who stopped by, as was his habit, conveniently before supper, with the words—timely, true, and ungrammatical—"Reverend Hickman ain't home." In the archway of that front hall I see our second son, John, about a year old, sitting in his canvas jump swing, bouncing up and down and laughing with delight at the attentions of the members of the Youth Fellowship who had come that Saturday afternoon to help us with the Sunday bulletins.

In that house I imagine that there are still, beneath the flooring of the smallest bedroom, a pair of blue snap-on toy truck wheels, dropped one afternoon (through the too-large circular hole that had been cut for the passage of a radiator pipe) by a small boy who could never retrieve them—nor could we. But whenever we asked Peter what had become of his missing truck wheels he would shake his head mournfully and say, "Lost in da pipes," an expression that has since become a family byword to express the mysterious disappearance of almost anything at all.

In the back yard of that house were marvelous red raspberry bushes, and I for whom red raspberries are the favorite summer fruit found it a good omen that our first parsonage should provide us with such a bounty. We ate them by the dishful, gave them away, used them in muffins and pancakes and ice cream until the days of that first summer taxed even my ingenuity for new ways to eat red raspberries. The same back yard held a bearing grape arbor, so we had our own grape jelly, and, standing along the back walk, was a handsome line of pink and white peonies that did not suffer from my usually disastrous efforts to take care of flowers. From that back yard Peter wandered off one day, soon after we moved in and before we had installed our fence. After twenty minutes of frantic searching, first by us and then with the help of the alerted neighbors, he was discovered to be at the police station. Someone in the street below ours had spotted him as a lost child and trundled him off to the station, where an alert policeman thought he might be the son of the new Methodist minister in town and called to ask whether anybody was missing up on our avenue. Hoyt went down to the station to retrieve his

son and bring him home—a little sobered but well fed by a choco-
late bar, the sticky remains of which still clung to his fingers,
that one of the policemen had given him to take his mind off his
lost condition. When this story reached the ears of our friend the
Bishop, he remarked that many ministers' children ended up in
the police station but not usually when they were only a year and
a half old!

While we were living in that house we experienced our first
parsonage remodeling job. The old-fashioned and inconvenient
kitchen was done over, the pantry was made into a lavatory, and
—for good reason, with by now *three* small boys in the house—
a folding door was put across the archway to the study. Thinking
we could manage somehow, and not wanting to leave Hoyt to
fend for himself, I started out trying to stay in the house while
the renovation was in process—going to the neighbor's to bathe
the baby and to give us all some respite from the plaster-filled
air and the buzz of saws. But after a day of this we gladly accepted my mother-in-law's invitation to come down and bring
the children for a visit, and they and I went off for a leisurely
vacation until the work was done.

Through planning for that and other renovations, as well as
through living in several parsonages, we have acquired some conviction on what living arrangements seem to work best in family
parsonages. We like older houses—they are usually bigger and
more solidly constructed than new houses that can be purchased
with the same money. By the time a house has been standing
thirty years or so, it shows its true sturdiness: houses that were
not well built in the first place have lived most of their short but
flashy lives by the time they're thirty years old. Some of the
money saved by purchasing an old house can be put into re-

modeling, so that with imagination and good judgment one can have the best of both worlds—the sturdiness of an old house and some of the important modern features that go with a new one. A house that is not new can be run around in by children without anyone worrying about the first scratches on walls and floors; though we are certainly as careful—no more and no less—with any parsonage as we would be if the house were our own.

In remodeling, our stress is toward what functions best. Wall-to-wall carpeting seems a good investment in main living areas, for ease of maintenance, for warmth, for simple and orderly good looks, for sound-cushioning, and for freedom from forever straightening area rugs to lie evenly with the grain of the floor. We hope for four bedrooms, though the house we now live in has only three, and our three boys share the single large bedroom running across the front of the house. Closet space matters, and somewhere for the children to play when someone comes to talk quietly with their father. We are for laundry space on the same level as the kitchen, if it can be managed at all, as a great saver of steps and to allow for smooth coordination of several household chores at once; you can put in a load of wash while waiting for the cookies to bake. We are for at least two bathrooms—always and forever—though old-fashioned fixtures, if they work and are reasonably easy to clean, do not bother us at all. Houses of thirty years' vintage date from an era when a second bathroom was not considered a necessity by many builders, but there is usually an extra pantry, or closet, or enclosable porch that can be converted to this use. Of course this, as all remodeling, costs money, and often the minister's family sees its needs as more urgent than does the relevant church committee. I have suggested to Hoyt that he shorten this time gap by earmarking wedding and funeral fees, traditionally his but which he always turns over to the church memorial fund, as funds for parsonage remodeling, "because you know we need another bathroom." "Yes," he says, "and we could call it the 'All Saints' Memorial Bathroom' " —thus ending any serious intention in *that* discussion.

Our second parsonage, to which we moved as a family of five, soon to be six, was a wide yellow brick house, set slightly back from the major U.S. highway that passed the front yard and with a farmyard bordering the deep back yard, in what was virtually a crossroads town in southwestern Pennsylvania. It was a wonderful layout for a family with young children. For the first time we had a family room—a sunny large room off the dining room and kitchen, at the opposite end of the house from the living room. We were able for the first time to have a laundry room by the kitchen. And the back yard, which ran in a long shallow slope up to the farmyard fence, was a splendid place to play. There was enough flat space by the house for a swing set, a children's swimming pool, and a sturdy clothesline; up the slope toward the fence was a low apple tree, beneath which we put our sandbox, and down this gentle hill the children could run and roll and, in the winter, ride on their small sleds. Beyond the back yard were the farmer's friendly cows and a flock of geese, which, each spring that we were there, produced a train of tiny goslings.

But all was not idyllic in this country setting. The house had terrible window and door fittings—there were no screens for the windows and only patched and loose-fitting screens for the doors, and the presence of the farmyard encouraged a booming bug population. For the first several weeks of our occupancy of the house, we kept spray cans of insect killers and repellants on the ready. The nearness of the farm and the country brought us other woodsy treats. On one of our early days in the house I came down the stairs and found Hoyt crouched over a garter snake which had somehow slithered into the front hall and which he was trying to get out of the house before I should see it. Another day a bat clung to the outer jamb of the back door and I slipped in and out quickly, so as not to let the bat into the house, until Hoyt came home and, upon going to remove the bat, found that it was dead.

The racket of the highway took some getting used to, as well as extra safety precautions for the children. The first night we were there neither Hoyt nor I slept at all. After that we hardly ever heard the night noises of cars and trucks steadily going by. But we could never sit out on the front porch without having the deafening traffic in our ears. And of course we had to be very careful lest the children wander toward the whizzing cars on the road.

Before we had lived in the house many weeks we got new screens for the windows and doors, and the big back yard was enclosed with fencing and a gate, and I was able to relax about the children and the bugs before our fourth child and first daughter was born and we brought her home to occupy the smallest bedroom, which we had—this time as a gesture of hope and in defiance of statistical prognosis—again painted pink.

But one other unidyllic feature showed up before our first summer was over, and it challenged our ingenuity, patience, and tact. We had not lived in the parsonage many weeks before we traced the mysterious bites with which our children became afflicted to some flat brown creatures we observed from time to time around the floor moldings of one of the bedrooms. A friend

identified them as bedbugs. Bedbugs! Not wishing to reflect on
the cleanliness of our predecessors or start what would certainly
be a "hot" news item in this little town—that the Methodist
parsonage had bedbugs—we invested quietly in those insect-
killing products that included in the small print on the can the
information that bedbugs were among the creatures this product
would kill. We sprayed, smeared, and otherwise distributed
several dollars' worth of insecticide. The bedbugs—and the bites
—disappeared, and we breathed easily again. But after our first
winter and with the coming of the warm spring, the bedbugs
again began to emerge from the floor boards. We surmised that
there must have been eggs dormant, which had now hatched, and
we again spread our lethal potions generously around, still hoping to avoid any scandal in a community which, like most
small communities, was ever eager for choice news items to talk
about. But after minor reprieves each time, the bedbugs came
back—in small numbers, to be sure, but any bedbugs is too many
bedbugs! I called an exterminator in the nearest city and talked
with the secretary. She assured me we would never get rid of
them without a professional job, and I was in no mood to argue.
Furthermore, the exterminating job would cost much more than
Hoyt and I had any intention of paying to rectify a condition
which should never have existed in the first place and for which
we certainly were not responsible. So, one summer Sunday after
church, an emergency meeting of the trustees having been called,
I came before them to present my plea. I described the emerg-
ings of the bedbugs, our efforts to handle the problem quietly
ourselves, related my conversation with the exterminating company, and declared, politely but firmly, that we had now had
enough of bedbugs and something more must be done.

The trustees were aghast and acquiescent. We arranged that the job be done while our family was away on vacation; the exterminator had recommended that the house be unoccupied for several days to ensure a safe and efficient job. We went away, and on our return and for the rest of our two years in that town —no more bedbugs.

I would not feel free to relate this series of incidents, lest people who know us hold our parsonage antecedents in that town in less esteem, were it not for the fact that the spring after *we* left the parsonage the bedbugs reappeared and the whole job had to be done over—this time, I am told, with greater attention to the bug-nesting potential of the unused and unventilated crawl space that stretched above the upstairs. And while that community has had other flurries of excitement whirling around the parsonage and its parade of inhabitants, to the best of my knowledge the incident of the bedbugs has added no fuel to any fire.

There have been several other houses. One, a rambling white frame house, which the church bought as its "new" parsonage while my husband was its minister, seemed home to me from the minute I first stepped through its door—a house with a white fireplace in the living room and with evergreen trees outside its windows and red cardinals to flash in season in those trees—in many respects so like the home I had grown up in that it was a peculiar wrench to leave it.

The one bizarre feature of this favored house was its upstairs bathroom. The bathroom was finished in orange and black wallboard and tile, which was all right if you needed a stimulating shock in the morning but wasn't too soothing if you should wander in with a queasy stomach or in search of an aspirin. The bathroom had a built-in electric wall heater, and a huge mirror covered the inside of the bathroom door—luxury features that suggested no economy-minded church committee had designed its decor. But the mirror did not, alas, survive our tenure in the house. One day one of the children left the wall heater running, and the mirrored door stood back against the heater long enough for the glass to expand and crack with a terrible bang. We offered to pay for the mirror's replacement, but after conferring with the parsonage committee we all agreed it was a rather narcissistic and hazardous spot for a mirror anyway, so we finished the raw wood with paint. I understand that the garish bathroom walls have been redone, and I feel—though it is none of my business—a little sorry to have them go; they were so refreshingly atypical of the usual pleasantly conservative furnishings of parsonages.

There was an upended matchbox of a house—four stories high, but with a floor space so small that with a single plugging in of the vacuum cleaner I could reach any point in any room on that floor. There was a house—the house scheduled for demolition—which almost refuted my previously held belief that we could never find a house too big for us. The house was not really too big, but it was dark, and it was awkward. Useless additional attic spaces opened off the backs of rooms; long halls had to be traversed to get to rooms around another corner, when a simpler arrangement would have allowed for cross-ventilation of the upstairs, and light, and a reasonable relationship of the walls of one room to the walls of another. As it was, nothing seemed to adjoin anything else, but rooms meandered off on their dark and incommunal ways, and you could not have any sense of the house as a coordinated and understandable dwelling.

There is the house we live in now—a sturdy, rather elegant

house, with leaded glass at the living room windows and fine oak woodwork—a homey kind of house. I think it will stand here for a long time, since before it became a parsonage it had stood through the tenure of several sets of owners. The house is large for the rather small lot it sits on, but we do not need a big yard at this stage of our family's life, and we have room enough for a small but secluded back lawn, and for flowers, and for mint and sage and chives and whatever experimental gardens the children are trying this year—corn, or cantaloupe, or giant radishes. The house has a big sunroom across the front of the first floor, with French doors to close the room off from the living room when someone wants to come and talk privately, and at the back of the house there is another "extra" room—a den—shared by a television set, the sewing machine, my desk, a hide-a-bed couch, an encyclopedia and some other books, the fish and the turtles.

This house has a stairway that divides halfway down: one half is carpeted with the green of the living room and goes to it, and the other half descends into the kitchen. This double stairway, which I thought at first was a waste of space, is one of the great conveniences of the house and a source of many extra options to the children who play here, our own and their friends, who come here and invariably comment on the possibilities of stairs like this—"Head him off at the pass!" and the like. The house has a huge garage—the man who built it had some kind of workshop there—that will house two cars, four sleds and four bicycles, a lawn mower, a cooking grill, and all manner of other items, and on its sturdy rafters our children have put wide boards to create a hideout, reachable only by ladder. By what whimsical chain of circumstances I do not know, the garage has on one side a stained glass window, and it gives me a kind of quaint pleasure to have this liturgical symbol in our Methodist parsonage garage.

The house has also a large and usable attic, as have the other houses where we have lived most happily. I would like to climb on my soapbox and declare myself as very much "for" attics. An attic is a good omen. An attic is a Put Now, Decide Later place. An attic is (if you are that kind of person) an organized junk pile. An attic is a realm of mystery, cobwebs, romance, and poor lighting—a remembrance of things past, a symbol of faith in future seasons and generations. Attics are not only good as storage places for out-of-season clothing and furniture we may need again, or as insulation from the sun in summer, or as a different and slightly adventurous environment for children to play in on a rainy day, or, if you have an old extra mattress you can keep on the floor, as emergency extra sleeping quarters. An attic stands for something, and I wonder whether, in our mobile and youth-oriented society, the fact that most houses are built without attics does not penalize us in ways that have little to do with convenience or lack of it. An attic is a place to store items that are not only valuable in themselves but as symbols of values not consciously with us all the time but to which it is to our advantage to return: a few choice baby clothes to pass along to the next generation of mothers, to wonder that a father could ever have had feet that small; a velvet gown—of no practical use to anyone as castoff clothing—which speaks to young daughters of their mother's courtship days and of a college dance at which their parents were the gay and tremulous young people they know themselves to be now; an old rocker that may be renovated some day but which even in its decrepitude stands for the hours during which three generations of mothers have rocked their babies.

Perhaps because my own growing years are so richly marked with attic associations, I mount my soapbox and hope for houses with attics. I remember the twice-yearly cleanings which my mother gave to our attic, and the sense of a rich past that came out with the smell of mothballs on the pile of old woolens in the trunk—baby capes, brocaded dresses, a well-worn quilt. The pictures of my father, young, valiant, and very handsome in his World War I uniform, tell of a time and a man we did not know but who speaks to us now. Some pictures of my mother and grandmother off for a summer's stay in the country, by horse and carriage if you will. I wonder now whether my allusions to a childhood that lives like yesterday in my mind connote to my children the same air of dim and unknowable past that my mother's stories of her trips to Taborton brought to my childhood mind. Is a childhood without television as remote to my children as my mother's trips in a horse-drawn buggy were to me? How valiantly we need to retain for others the immediacy of ourselves as children. And how hard it is.

In the drawers of old clothing, in our twice-yearly coursings through the attic, we would come upon a pair of long hatpins, with a small fierce Indian head cast in bronze holding the eight-inch shaft of each pin, and I remember the inner start with which I heard my mother say that women used to use these not only to hold flat velvet hats on high-piled coiffures but to "protect themselves," and no P.T.A. film on the dangers of fraternizing with strangers could begin to assume the dramatic proportions of the scenes those hatpins brought to mind. There was a chest of old papers—college themes of my mother's—and another of my father's youthful memorabilia, including a small heartbreaking box labeled "George's baby work—age 3," which contained small pieces of cloth marked out with rows of tiny stitches, made at what cost to the cramping of small muscles and the frustrations of a little boy and at what dutiful urgings of my grandmother, a woman of aristocratic and old-fashioned New England, we could only imagine. There was a drawer that held sewing scraps, put away for future patches or quilt pieces, and one of the attic-cleaning diversions was to find the rolls of scraps that went with favorite dresses and to observe how the scraps were still bright though some of the dresses had faded. There was a chest of our baby clothes, and a drawer with a few choice quilts and baby clothes that had been our parents—with long trailing skirts, dresses crusted with handmade embroidery and fragile with inserts of handmade lace, tiny ruffled silk bonnets, and long white baby stockings.

But of all the treasures that the attic held, there was none that could compare with what lay inside the gray box labeled "Kenwood Mills." The box had originally contained a pair of blankets with which my parents had started out their life together, but on those days when, at the end of our cleaning sprees, we watched as my mother opened the box, we saw first sheafs of wrinkled blue tissue paper and then, beneath them, an armful of white veiling, limp and wrinkled but still beautiful, attached to a circle of handmade lace and dried orange blossoms. And under that, the dress itself—our mother's wedding dress—creamy satin and seed pearls, low-waisted in the fashion of 1922, short-skirted but with a long wide panel of train that, my mother explained to us, "fell from the shoulders here"—an ivory cascade of dress, and of romance, and of beginning, and of past, and of us. In the corner of the box were her shoes—pointed white kid shoes fastened with a buttoned instep strap—and a hand-woven garter of pale blue. The box was never tied up tight, but we never opened it on those many other days of hurried trips and play in the attic, just on those special days of sorting and cleaning and repiling and remembering. I am familiar with the custom of brides today of having a wedding gown hermetically sealed and untouchable after a wedding, with maybe a cellophane window to peer through. This is to preserve the dress—for a daughter, probably, against the dust and handling of the years. But I would choose instead, as a gift of love to my daughter, to put my wedding dress in a big box, with lots of tissue paper and a lid that lifts off, so that on occasions of our choosing the dress and veil could be drawn forth, and turned to the light, and looked at, and the occasion of its wearing remembered or imagined and, in either case, held in love.

The dress would survive, as my mother's did. When I came to be married myself it was my mother's wedding dress, remade to me, that I chose to wear. It was not only the cream-colored satin that went with me down the aisle but the remembrance of blue tissue paper and cracked and softened veil, of dried orange blossoms and white kid shoes, and all the bright spring days in which my sister and I, surrounded by the mystery of the past and the love of our mother, had helped to clean the attic.

Our parsonage attic now is tenanted by many things, though we try not to save things thoughtlessly. (One of my family slogans is "When in doubt, throw it out.") There are the few pieces of furniture that do not fit this house but may fit in some other. There are the things we have kept for sentimental reasons: some pictures, a few clothes of the children's and our own—the same wedding dress that hallowed my parents' attic, Hoyt's "director's coat" and his Navy uniform. There are the scraps of cloth. There are the Christmas ornaments, including a small composition camel that was injured when, thirty years ago, summer lightning tore into the attic of my parents' home and struck a chip from the camel's side as he lay in the box marked "manger set."

We have in our attic a truly splendid collection of old Methodist books, arranged in several glass-fronted bookcases. They are really too good to be in an attic, but we do not have room for them in the main part of the house. They are safe here, and they lend a certain dignity to our attic and affirm us, even here, as the book lovers we are.

We have in our attic some standard items of baby furniture we no longer need. Some we have given away, but some we have kept for visiting nieces and nephews and friends, and when these have grown we shall still keep these items for a time of future grandchildren—a time that will probably seem to be upon us with incredible speed.

In the attic are the seasonal changes of clothes. Along with the turning of leaves in the fall and the need to remove storm windows in the spring, the seasonal changes of the clothes is a good ritual with which to mark the passing times of year—the exchange of the ponderousness of winter and winter clothing for the light bright time and clothing of summer, the boots traded for the beach sandals, the ear muffs for the sun hats. This change of climate, particularly from summer and fall to winter, is a change many people bemoan, but we would miss it were it not a part of our life, and the attic is a good scene against which to play out the business of these changes as they come and go and come again.

So, I would wish for parsonages with attics. A living room can be dark or light, a kitchen can be old-fashioned or modern, a house can have three bedrooms or four, but an attic is an attic forever!

VII
The Public Life of a Private Person

Most ministers' wives think of themselves, I believe, as basically private persons; or, as someone has put it, "The best minister's wife is the best wife to the minister."

But all of us know that because of our husbands' positions as pastors of churches we are also slightly public persons, fight it as we may. And fight it we do! The slogan, "Be yourself!" gets an emphatic cluck of approval from any group of ministers' wives engaging in this aspect of husband shoptalk, and we talk a great deal about breaking out of the stereotype with which we may think we are shackled. But the reality of our double identity will win in the end. We wear red hats or we do not wear red hats or we do not wear hats at all; we go to dances or we do not go to dances; we disclose our husbands' vocation or we try, in new groups, *not* to let our husbands' vocation be known until first we are known—and all of these decisions we make instinctively in the context of ourselves both as private persons and as ministers' wives. Whether we like it or not, we walk a kind of swaying tightrope among the various pressures and attractions which affect us as slightly public persons.

But where, in this vast sea, the tightrope swings, is of our choosing. At least it is if we are blessed, as I am, with a husband who has sufficient freedom and security about his own vocation to let me choose my own way, too; and, if, of course, our tastes and life styles are not incompatible with our husbands' deepest intention as ministers. I say deepest intention. I have no patience for those demands of superficial conformity which some ministers' wives in the past seem to have felt themselves constrained to abide by; fine points of housekeeping, dress, and decorum are just not matters for public decision, and a minister's wife, especially today, who feels herself threatened by what she estimates is a congregation's pressure on unimportant matters is telling more about her own insecurity as a person than about the unrealistic demands of others. If, of course, the minister's wife, either in word or action, proclaims herself as out of sympathy with her husband's being a Christian minister at all, there is probably trouble ahead. But for a woman who has moderate emotional health, and whose assumptions about life are not at cross-purposes with her husband's, the direction of the swing of her own particular tightrope can be one of the challenges and delights of her life, and I suppose there is nowhere that a minister's wife reveals more of her feelings about herself as a person than in the degree of tautness and sway she allows to herself as a slightly public person and the hesitancy or zest with which she advances her foothold.

A good share of the public life of a minister's wife plays itself out in the organizations of the church of which her husband is pastor. What shall she do in the local church? A few ministers' wives adopt as a platform that they will take no responsibility for leadership in the church life. A few others—and these will probably get in a greater complex of hot water than the total abstainers, because church ladies' groups have their share of prima donnas already—will feel they must be Sidewalk Superintendent if not Chief Engineer of everything pertaining to women that goes on in the church, and V.I.P. observer of everything else. Most of us find our place somewhere between these two extremes.

A favorite spot for the minister's wife to be asked to serve is as Secretary of Spiritual Life in the Woman's Society: she must be "spiritual"—her husband is the minister. If she demurs on this one, or if the church is wise enough to entrust this responsibility to someone whose husband is not a minister, a good second spot for the minister's wife is as Secretary of Missionary Education and Service. Most women's societies have some guilt feelings about their lack of real emotional investment in "foreign" missions (after all, has not the real purpose of the woman's society, at least historically, been to bring life to the alien heathen?) and perhaps the minister's wife can help the ladies with their lethargic zeal. The more "worldly" jobs, which means the money-raising jobs, she is seldom asked to do, which suits her just fine, and she is happy, this once, not to disturb the pedestal on which she is put as the minister's wife and therefore a "spiritual" person. She can reinstate herself as a "real" person by baking bread for the bazaar, telling stories of her children's misbehavior, and complaining that her husband, like everybody else's husband, forgets to tell her things he is assumed to have told her—that there is to be a coffee hour after church this Sunday, or that he is to be out of town for three days next week, or that on the day she always does her grocery shopping he has agreed to leave the car for state inspection.

Contrary to the impression given by the amount of attention it receives, the Woman's Society is not the only organization in the church that involves women. There is the Sunday school. Unless the church of which one's husband is minister is very large, chances are that someone will, after a decent interval, approach the minister's wife about teaching a Sunday school class. A common spot for her seems to be as a teacher in some department of the Children's Division. Ministers' wives like children, don't they, and it is comfortable for all to picture the minister's wife in sweet communion with children, with perhaps the slight executive responsibility of a superintendency thrown in. Probably she will not be nursery superintendent—that is considered, except by those who work in the nursery department, an easy job, and for it there may be many volunteers. Nor will she, unless she is very intrepid and skillful, thrust herself into the maelstrom of youth classes, as everyone knows you have to be a combination of judge, hippie, and sports buff to succeed as a Sunday school teacher in the Youth Division, and that does not describe most people's idea of a minister's wife.

The Adult Division, perhaps? The Adult Division will probably be well supplied with favorite teachers of long standing. Besides, the adults are considered to be already established in the Christian life, and it would be wasting the services of such a "spiritual" person as the minister's wife to have her teaching the pillars of the church. Back to the Children's Division with her—unless she, having small children at home all week, is fed to the teeth with child patter and orientation and can prevail on the Sunday School Superintendent to let her have a try at perceptive, exasperating, and idealistic tenth-graders.

Some ministers' wives like to sing in the choir, and the musical life of the church is another favorite spot for the minister's wife to make her pitch. Having been in the no-self-confidence column of college choirs myself, and never having felt free to assign an evening a week to choir practice, I have sat that one out, enjoying the music from a distance and feeling slightly envious of those women who could sing with melodious and undiverted attention while I tried to preserve an apparently effortless peace in the pew among my own four children and perhaps a couple of their friends of equally wiggly proclivities.

In addition to the Woman's Society, the Sunday school, and some of the more esoteric arms of church life in which the minister's wife may function as a slightly public person, there are, in any community, several other organizations who will consider a minister's wife a natural affiliate to their group, and who will seek her out, sometimes sight unseen and conviction untested, to join up with them. In Protestant churches in which abstinence from alcoholic beverages is known to be part of the church's official platform, such an organization is the Women's Christian Temperance Union or, as it is known, the W.C.T.U. The W.C.T.U., partly through its own ineptitude and partly through the unremitting efforts of its enemies (whose livelihood is frequently at stake), has come upon hard times. A new minister's wife in town is viewed by a local chapter of the W.C.T.U. as a hoped-for infusion of new life, and she is approached by the membership chairman with the tentative eagerness with which penguins are said to offer stones to each other as gestures of courtship. To join or not to join?—that is the question. I did join, to give encouragement to the ladies in an unpopular cause for which I have some sympathy, and as a kind of conservative counterbalance to some of the more radical activities which I also support, and, I suppose, because I had no very good reason *not* to join. I try to talk fast if one of my friends looks at me with a reproachful and incredulous eye when I admit to membership in this subversive group, but I must say that I have been pleasantly surprised at the quality of the programs of the few meetings I have attended. At one meeting a very competent young woman spoke on her work at a center for the shelter and rehabilitation of alcoholics, which center reflected the most advanced and compassionate understanding of alcohol problems. At another meeting a school man spoke about tobacco and alcohol education in the public schools, a subject in which I as a parent had great interest, though the high point of that meeting came during the worship service when we were all joined in singing "The Battle Hymn of the Republic." This hymn had not been the one called for by the worship leader, but the pianist had misunderstood the page number and had launched into the Battle Hymn with such fervor that the group had no choice but, after a moment of helpless fumbling, to sing along. Having got off to such a bad start, we were redoubling our effort, and midway through the song a chart of a thermometer whose rising red line indicated the number of members who had finally paid up their dues detached itself from the wall of the living room where we were meeting and, with a great flap and clatter, fell to the floor beside the startled visiting speaker, while his truth went marching on.

The local Council of Churches, apart from its identity with the local church of which her husband is pastor, may also see in the minister's wife a qualified person to participate in its varied activities. These can range from committees on cooperative Leadership Education schools, to occasions of Catholic-Protestant dialogue, to vehicles for aiding underprivileged persons with goods and services, to holding a really swinging party for nearby migrant workers.

Another group that will eye the minister's wife as a prospective member of special value is the P.T.A. Presumably the minister's wife, if she has children currently in public school, will want to join the P.T.A. anyway, but upon joining she will also become one of those few persons considered qualified to be the Third Vice-President—which, being translated, means devotional chairman. Now anyone of humane intent and moderate poise could be devotional chairman. "Devotions" usually consist of some brief humanitarian reading, and newspapers, magazines, and books abound with appropriately nonsectarian homilies or prayers. But evidently many women, though they may be quite active in their local churches or synagogues, would as soon do a striptease as to express any religious feeling in a public forum.

The minister's wife who contemplates the job is not without qualms, either. For one thing she is likely to be very sensitive about not inflicting her particular denominational slant upon the membership, many of whom are non-Christian, let alone non-Methodist, Lutheran, or Episcopalian. Besides that sensitivity, there is the whole question of the propriety of religious devotions at school meetings at all. Ministers and their wives, to the apparent surprise of other people, are often among the staunchest defenders of the controversial Supreme Court decision on "establishment of religion" in public schools: in addition to the questionable ethics and constitutionality of the schools' getting into the act on matters of religious devotion in a pluralistic setting, there is the practical fact that whereas other families may need to look to the schools to bolster in their children a weak religious identification, at least ministers' families do not have *that* problem.

But all this misgiving notwithstanding, the minister's wife, as having little to lose, is the most likely candidate for the job, and, like President Kennedy being extra careful not to lay himself open to the charge of favoritism toward Catholicism, the Protestant minister's wife will probably present the most broadly based series of readings from Horace Mann, Socrates, and Thoreau ever to go under the name of "Devotions." A reading from Pope John or Martin Buber, possibly. But Paul Tillich—well, hardly ever.

There will be other groups who will turn to the minister's wife as to a person of assured public spirit. Various charitable and service organizations may, for instance, ask her to serve on their boards of directors or help them in some other capacity. A minister's wife will do well to have done some sounding in a community before she accepts these invitations. Some of these groups, while they do perform good service to a community, function mainly as social units, and the newspaper accounts of annual meetings will be on the social page of the paper, with full attention to who wore what and little space given to any services voted or discussed. Not that there is anything wrong in social life connected with good causes, but it is well to know what one is getting into.

There are also educational and interest groups to which the minister's wife may be invited and which she may choose to join for her own enrichment. In some ways these groups are particularly helpful to a minister's wife because she comes to them primarily as a private person, not as a public figure. A minister's-wife friend with whom I was talking at a meeting of the American Association of University Women said to me, "I feel like a person when I come here," and the same could be said for other groups—reading groups, art groups, drama groups—to which a woman comes bringing as her "entrance requirements" her own talent and experience and not the fact that her husband is a minister and she is therefore assumed to be welcome, interested, and valuable. Though even here, she will do well not to expect complete impunity—she will be asked to give the Invocation at the Christmas dinner or to be a committee member of the study group on Ethical Values, or someone may come up to her and say, "What special interest groups do you ministers' wives like to join?" as though we had a common mind and taste. Or she will find herself juggling the value to her of being in a musical comedy the local drama group is putting on against the possible damage she might do to the image of the minister's family if she appears in a red satin costume with black mesh tights. But these little uprisings are very small disturbances in the rhythm with which the minister's wife, in groups of this kind, is able, if she tries, to walk to her own particular music.

I suppose most of us think of our taste in matters of art, music, films, and literature as being private matters, but here, too, if we are people to whom expressions of artistic taste are important, the line between the publicly perceived taste and the private person is very hard to hold. I was once reproached after church by a lady who told me she understood I had taken from the library a book by Norman Mailer, and why was I reading "books like that"? I wondered how she had acquired this piece of information, as I am not in the habit of making public announcements about what I am reading. Then I remembered that the woman in the library from which I had withdrawn the book was a member of the church and had evidently, though she had said nothing about it to me, been disturbed by my choice and had called my accuser to share her feelings. We had a pleasant though mutually astonished conversation there at the back of the church, I trying to explain my interest in and taste for modern literature as a meaningful exploration of life, and she trying to predict disastrous social consequences from the endorsement one gave to such books by reading them. After a few minutes we parted, with good will and with our own convictions on what Christians "should" read even stronger than before.

So much for some of the common areas where a minister's wife finds herself, whether she wishes it or not, assuming the stature of a public figure. There is another arena of activity, and it is considered more fraught with danger than a dictatorship in the Woman's Society, or overzealousness in the P.T.A., or a taste for obscure poetry. I refer to the political arena, to which, as the saying goes, let us now turn.

VIII
Citizens for Citizens

My career in politics was short and exhilarating. I got in on my husband's reputation. Before the 1960 election my husband supported Kennedy for President—not from the pulpit but, when he was asked, in private conversation. Until recently it has been something of an eyebrow-raiser for upper-middle-class Protestants to be Democrats at all, at least in "nonintellectual" circles; before the 1960 election it was practically a show-stopper for a Protestant minister to support Kennedy—at least in the small Pennsylvania city where we lived. So that what began as private conversations soon became public knowledge, and my husband, as a Protestant minister of known Democratic conviction, became, for the Democrats, a "find."

Because of this we began to receive a succession of racy invitations to Democratic functions—annual banquets, installations of officers, pep dinners—at which my husband was asked to give the invocation or benediction; a rabbi or a priest was usually on hand for the other of these ceremonies. (It is an interesting commentary on group mores that people seem to feel uneasy if somebody doesn't bless the food at mass public meals, even though probably very few of the people present have any tradition of asking grace before meals in their own homes. After all, if you don't have a blessing how do you know when it is polite to begin eating? And, with somewhat less urgency, if you don't have a benediction, how do you conclude the meeting with style?)

Well, we went to the dinners, enjoying a milieu somewhat different from that of the usual run of church functions, and we were as jubilant as any other supporters when Kennedy won the election.

It was when the 1962 election began to loom that my career had its brief and brilliant flowering.

We had a neighbor who, in addition to being the mother of some of our children's playmates, was vice-chairman of the county Democratic party. One morning in the fall of 1962 I got a call from her telling me that I would be getting another call (this call about the call became standard diplomatic procedure), inviting me to a select luncheon at the local hotel the next noon. (If my husband was a "find," so, by extension, was I.) The meeting was to talk over the possibility of opening a local chapter of Citizens for Clark-Dilworth. Senator Clark was up for re-election in Pennsylvania and Mr. Dilworth was running for governor, both on the Democratic ticket. At the lunch there would be two women from Pittsburgh: one a professional organizer for Citizens for Clark-Dilworth and the other a co-chairman of the region which included our city. There would also be several prominent men from town who were not publicly active in the Democratic party but who were eager to see Clark and Dilworth elected. My neighbor assured me my acceptance of the lunch invitation would in no way commit me to being active on the tentative committee if I didn't want to be. I had four young children and a very busy husband and didn't feel I should take on a lot of extra duties. I said yes, I would go.

In due time the second call came. The purpose of the lunch was described to me again, and again I said yes, I would go. Fine. I was to go to the lobby of the hotel at a few minutes before twelve the next day and I'd find the two women there. How would I know them? The professional lady had dark hair drawn back straight into a bun.

The next day I got to the hotel and looked in through the big glass doors. I could see the two women sitting on a sofa and facing the other way. They were both wearing black, and looked very high-minded and chic. Neither of them had on a hat. I was wearing pink, and a hat. I took the hat back to the car; then I went into the lobby. I walked over to the women, tentatively. I felt I should hum "Londonderry Air," as they did in a spy story I read, when unknown agents identified themselves to each other. The women got up and greeted me cordially and we all sat down again. They asked me about any previous experience I had had in political activity. The best I could come up with was that I had made some calls on behalf of Stevenson in the fall of 1952 and that my husband as a student at Haverford had done some ward work for Mr. Dilworth when he was running for District Attorney of Philadelphia. These were not exactly major qualifications, but they did show that our hearts had been in the right place for several years.

The men began to arrive: an optometrist who was head of the school board, a local architect, a dentist, a man who worked at the radio station, a couple of businessmen who were active in city life. I had met several of them before, though I knew none of them well. We were all introduced.

The manager of the hotel appeared and was introduced all around. He said our room was ready, and we all went up in the elevator to a small private dining room, where a table was set in the best private dining room style—linen and crystal and ash trays, and easy chairs around the fireplace. I thought of my children feasting on canned beans at home.

I sat by the other two women, and the men spread themselves around the rest of the table. Another man arrived—a young businessman who was active in our church. We were introduced and nodded discreetly to each other. I don't know whether he was more surprised to see me or I to see him, but I suspect the former.

We ordered lunch. The Pittsburgh ladies ordered first. They ordered salads—one of the cheaper items on the menu. I ordered the same thing, not wanting to spend too much of the Cause's money, either. The men were less cautious. When it came to dessert, the ladies passed that, too. I said I wouldn't have any dessert, either. The men had dessert. At the end of the meal someone suggested we save money for the Committee and pay for our own lunches. Then someone else suggested that for simplicity's sake we divide the check equally among us, rather than try to figure out each person's share. I was learning about politics the hard way.

After lunch we got down to business. Yes, we all agreed that we'd like to have a Citizens for Clark-Dilworth in our county. There were many people who, like most of us, were not active in party politics but would be happy to do what they could for the election of Senator Clark and Mr. Dilworth. The professional lady from Pittsburgh, the one with the chic black hair, began to ask each man if he would be willing to be chairman of a citizens' group. One by one they all demurred—they would love to, but they had business trips coming up, or were just too busy right now, or, in the case of the radio man, he was too actively identified with the Democratic party to be an effective citizens' chairman. But they would all help; they would do everything they could: they just couldn't be chairman. I remarked that this sounded like a church gathering. No one asked me to be chairman—a good thing, as I was neither qualified nor willing. Eventually they discussed the possibility that another man, absent that day, might be prevailed on to be chairman. One of the men agreed to ask him.

The matter of a chairman thus disposed of, we discussed a headquarters. The radio man said that we could have the use of a hotel room, free. The intended room wasn't on the street level —a decided disadvantage—but it was free. I think it was some kind of deal he had made with the hotel manager: if the hotel got to serve one of the coming large banquets, the manager would let the Citizens have the use of a headquarters room. We were also to be allowed to string large banners from the hotel marquee, saying "Citizens for Clark-Dilworth," and this would partly compensate for the relative obscurity of the room itself.

The election was about six weeks away. We agreed that we should open the headquarters about three weeks before election. We also agreed on the date for a public meeting to enlist support for the Citizens for Clark-Dilworth. Throughout this discussion I tried to look intelligent but took little part. I did enjoy the thought of my housewifely self in this caucus-y atmosphere. It was easily worth the price of the lunch.

One by one the men had to go, and as they went they vowed their support. One of the older men, on departure, made a flowery speech to me to the effect that his wife, when she had been my age, looked as good as I did now, and he hoped that when I became her age I'd look as good as she did now. It was a little involved but I was glad about the pink. I would certainly do what I could for Messrs. Clark and Dilworth.

Finally the radio man and the two ladies from Pittsburgh and I were left. As if by common consent one of the ladies asked me if I would be willing to be in charge of the headquarters. Aha! I asked what that would involve, as I wouldn't be able, with my four children and my minister husband, to spend a great deal of time away from home. I could spend some time in the mornings, but my youngest child was only in kindergarten and I would have to be home in the afternoons.

Well, could I set up the schedule, block out a chart, and contact people to be at the headquarters for certain hours? The men would give me lots of help with names of people who would probably be willing to work. I could do most of this by telephone, and from home. I enjoy making charts, I was interested in the cause, and the exhilaration of politics was already beginning to take hold. Yes, I would be glad to make up the schedule.

We conferred a little longer. The radio man gave me a beginning list of names to call. We agreed that it was important to preserve the image of the Citizens as being apart from the regular Democratic party, though I was assured the local party chairman would be most cooperative. I was to be known as the Office Coordinator of Citizens for Clark-Dilworth. I thought that, should I send this news in to my alumnae magazine (I never did), it would sound rather impressive, though not in a class with my contemporaries, who were always off on cultural missions to Bangkok or setting up advanced educational programs for women.

On my way home I stopped at the store and bought a spiral notebook. Thus armed I went home, announced my impressive title to my family, and began to block out my charts: three weeks of Mondays through Saturdays plus the Monday and Tuesday of election week; each day two three-hour shifts, of from two to five and from five to eight. Then I began calling the people whom I had been told would work at headquarters and who would know of others who would work. We had decided to have two people working together, and I had 120 man-hours to assign.

With each call I told my name, that I was calling for Citizens for Clark-Dilworth, that her name had been suggested as a worker, and would she be willing to help? I explained the hours headquarters would be open. If the person indicated he or she would work, we agreed on times. I asked whether she would like to bring someone to work with her or have me get someone. I invited each one to the general meeting, and to the official opening of the headquarters three weeks and a day before election.

Most of the names I had been given and was calling were "party regulars," and they couldn't have cared less about not confusing the image of the Citizens with that of the local Democratic party. They said, "Oh, sure, I always work." We couldn't have gotten along without them. They knew what to do at a headquarters. Many of them knew each other well. They told me who would work well with whom. They told me who were good workers but not too good at meeting the public, so put

them on at non-busy hours. They told me about their husbands'
sicknesses and their own fears of strange buildings. They were
affable and cooperative. One lady who I know had small children
told me she would work "anytime you need me" and referred to
the President of the United States as "a living doll."

The chart was beginning to have more filled-up spaces than
blank ones. The evening came for the public meeting to elicit
support for Citizens for Clark-Dilworth. My husband and I went.
The organizing lady from Pittsburgh was there and made a fer-
vent speech in behalf of the nominees. The local Democratic
party officials were there, and there was much verbal bowing and
scraping about our welcoming the efforts of each other, that we
were all working together for the good of the state and nation.
All the appropriate people were introduced. It seemed like a pep
meeting of one big uneasy family, with common good intentions
but a little nervous lest we pre-empt each other's prerogatives.

At the meeting we were asked to sign up to host a "coffee"
for which the Citizens would provide a speaker. My husband
and I made a hasty conferral and decided we could profitably
invite the local ministers to such an event; while many of them
might hesitate to engage in political discussion with parishioners, they might welcome the chance to talk things over with each
other and an informed speaker.

After the meeting we visited around, absorbing the air of growing enthusiasm for the cause and chatting with the party regulars
who had come to lend their slightly suspicious support.

During the next days I made calls and more calls. The Citizens
at last had co-chairmen. The man who'd been missing from the
lunch and therefore had been suggested had not been willing to
serve. But one of the businessmen and the young lawyer had

agreed to be co-chairmen. The lawyer agreed, in response to appeals from me, to provide the headquarters ladies with some useful work to do during such of their time as they weren't passing out buttons and brochures and answering questions. There were street lists they could go over and people to call to see if they needed rides to the polls. It was really party work and not Citizens work, but it was something worth doing and most of the ladies were party workers anyway.

We got the headquarters room set up—a better light, a few posters, some chairs, a couple of telephones, some reading matter, and that essential of all functioning offices, a hot plate.

The opening date was set for Monday morning. The Dean of the University of Pittsburgh Law School was state co-chairman of Citizens for Clark-Dilworth and was coming to town to officially open the headquarters. All the workers and other interested persons were invited to come. I was to be there and have my picture taken with the Dean and the young lawyer—the other co-chairman was away on a business trip. I began to get slightly cold feet. I called the lawyer and told him I was glad to help, and I would still come if he wanted me, but I didn't hanker for the publicity; the whole thing was a little unusual for a minister's wife, and if people saw my picture. . . . He said he appreciated my position, but he did think it would help the cause, so I agreed to come, picture and all. As someone said to me later, "There are so few respectable Democrats, Mrs. Hickman," and I was undeniably respectable.

When I got to the headquarters, the place was crowded. The cameramen were setting up. The Dean arrived and we were all introduced. Many of the women I'd called on the phone came over and introduced themselves to me and asked for last-minute instructions. The Dean and the lawyer and I were posed in front of a large poster of Clark and Dilworth halfway up a ladder, smiling and waving. Then we were arranged for another shot, while the attenders stood around and watched. Then the Dean made a short enthusiastic speech extolling Clark and Dilworth.

The local Bar Association was taking advantage of the Dean's presence in town to have him speak at a special lunch meeting, right after the headquarters opening. I was invited, and my husband, because of me. Usually I am invited places because of him.

At the lunch we sat across from the County District Attorney and his assistant. The Dean spoke to the lawyers about current developments at the law school. He told about the use of computers in legal research, and about a new course in law as it related to the European Common Market. To me, accustomed to the monthly meetings of the Woman's Society and the P.T.A., this was heady stuff. I almost wished I'd worn my Phi Beta Kappa key.

After the lunch I went back to the headquarters, checked out the first shift, and said the lawyer would be in soon to tell them what else to do. Then I went home and rechecked my charts.

About a week later Senator Clark came to town. There was a dinner meeting in the evening and he was to speak to a full house, but a few of us were to meet him briefly in the afternoon at headquarters. At the appropriate hour the select few assembled and waited. There was an approaching murmur, and steps along the hall, and Senator Clark and his entourage appeared. He was a friendly, moderately handsome man with a purposeful air. He had with him several Ivy League-ish attendants and a young woman. He introduced her. "This is my daughter, Noel, who's traveling with me." "Hello," she said, and nodded. She was a handsome girl, in a red dress, with her dark hair in a modified beehive. The Senator chatted for a few moments about the headquarters and the campaign, and then, with mutual good wishes and thanks, he and his group left.

Another day the Citizens sponsored a "coffee" in a private home, at which Mrs. Jonas Salk spoke on behalf of Clark and Dilworth. More picture-taking. Mrs. Salk was charming and effective. The other ladies seemed a little in awe of her. So was I, but I sat by her and talked with her anyway. My sister-in-law had been on a scientific program with her husband, and I told her how this had delighted the family. I thanked her on behalf of my children for her husband's work, and she seemed genuinely pleased. I wondered how many hundreds of times she'd had people tell her this and yet she was still gracious about it.

The businessman co-chairman of Citizens made a brief speech of welcome to Mrs. Salk and also extolled the candidates. His culminating remark was that both men were "Christian gentlemen—in the broad sense of the word." Since the hostess and many of the guests were Jewish, I thought this wasn't the best choice of complimentary generalities. I thought of a friend's remark, made some years before, that in some parts of our culture saying a person isn't a Christian is like saying he doesn't brush his teeth.

The headquarters ran smoothly through its three weeks and two days. I left a request on the desk that each afternoon's crew call the next day's workers to remind them of their hours, so we had relatively few gaps in the staff. The lawyer faithfully kept the ladies supplied with work. I dropped in occasionally to check on things and to chat, but for the most part I stayed with my family at home. If any of our church members objected to my active participation in politics, I didn't hear about it.

The election came. Senator Clark won the election; Mr. Dilworth did not. The Citizens for Clark-Dilworth ceased to exist, and the regular party carried on.

My political career was over, at least for now. With genuine relief I went back to dishes, washing, the Woman's Society, and the P.T.A. But when I see the District Attorneys' picture in the paper, or the County Commissioner's, I nod to myself and recall that they are my ex-cronies. When, as the local parades go by, one of these same political figures scans the faces of the crowds and his glance comes to me, he nods and waves, and I wave back and feel like a politico again.

And whenever someone says in my hearing, "A minister's wife should *never* go into politics," I think back on my days with the Citizens and, if my courage is high and it's that kind of day, I launch into my tale.

IX
Thirty-one Days, with
Four or Five Sundays

We are going to leave right after church, plus the few minutes necessary to eat lunch and finish packing the car. The children and I have gone to early service this Sunday, so we can get home and get changed and I can have lunch ready when Hoyt comes home soon after noon.

Most of the clothes packing was done yesterday, the boys assembling in jumbled heaps on their beds the items from the lists I have given them; Mary putting hers into neatly folded and stacked piles. Their really important things, which for lack of a better word we call "oddities," the children have had ready for a long time. The oddities may include a couple of books apiece from the public library (supposedly not to be read until vacation), cameras, flashlights, sunglasses, jackknives, plus whatever extra oddities the children consider necessary adjuncts to vacation.

Peter has collected all the fishing gear, plus a pocket book on angling and one on golf. John has his list of states—he is eager to check off some that he has never visited before—and his wallet and his Friendly Loan Company pad.

John saves his money, amassed from birthday gifts and allowance payments. The other children spend theirs. Then they come to John for a loan: he has established the Friendly Loan Company, at scandalously high interest rates, though he will reduce the rates for long-term loans if the prospective borrower is too hesitant. For a period of Stephen's affluence, he operated the Friendlier Loan Company, and the resulting price war made loans available at lower rates, but now John has no competition and the rates are back up. The family borrowers are glad enough to pay. Even Hoyt and I have borrowed money from John and paid the high rates willingly, as a tribute to John's thrift and to our need of cash. When the other children, spurred partly I am sure by jealousy and partly as a protest against a habit of thrift they cannot understand, ask John what he is saving for, he suggests, "My college education." "And then what?" they want to know. "My engagement ring." "And then what?" "My pension fund."

Stephen has a fishing tackle box of oddities—he refers to it as his "survival kit"—full of jars, booklets, empty pill containers, cotton balls, a compass, an outdoor thermometer, a small net on a twisted metal handle. And, in addition, two big books on biology and insects.

Mary has a selection of small dolls, and their clothes, a choice stuffed animal, a couple of paperbacks of "Peanuts" cartoons. At the last minute she brings out a boxed deluxe edition of Hans Christian Andersen fairy tales and says, "Can I take this? I'll carry it."

Hoyt comes home and we eat our lunch. I clean up as he finishes packing the car. Until recently we always packed our big suitcases on the roof of the station wagon, so we'd have the cargo space for "stretching room." But last year the rope holding the tarpaulin broke and pieces of our luggage went flying out behind us onto a Nebraska highway, at no damage to anyone and minimal damage to the luggage, but the possibilities for disaster were so ominous we are going to try our trip this year with everything packed inside.

Everyone has been instructed—or so we thought—to bring down his things and put them by the door. On a last-minute check through the house I find Mary's suitcase, closed and ready to go, lying on the middle of her bed. I rush down with it. Hoyt must take out half the contents of the cargo space to include Mary's suitcase in good position, and then repack it all.

We are ready at last. All we have to do is take the hamster and turtles to the church, where the understanding custodian will look out for them, take the guinea pigs to a friend's house, where the children of the family will care for our guinea pigs along with their own, take the goldfish to the neighbor's, and take the baby frogs back to the creek and let them go. We have also, after a last-minute appeal, promised the three younger children that they may have sunglasses for the vacation—they have reminded us that we paid half the expense last year of some good sunglasses for Peter. We go to the drugstore to pick up the Sunday *New York Times* (we will get it read *some*how) and to pick out, after many tryings-on, a pair of sunglasses apiece for John, Stephen, and Mary.

We get back in the car. Peter cannot find his sunglasses. He has looked in the appropriate place, he knows he put the sunglasses with his oddities—where could they be? He knows he checked his bed and his desk just before we left and the sunglasses were not there, either. The inference is that I must have mislaid them. We agree that if the sunglasses do not turn up within forty-eight hours we will buy Peter a new pair.

We have disposed of our animals, procured our new sunglasses, decided what to do about the missing sunglasses, and we start up again. Hoyt's theory of vacation is that it doesn't begin for him until he has passed the farthest point of the church's parish, and we are not there yet. He is getting understandably tense at all the delays. We are stopped for a red light. The traffic is thick. Peter sees a car with a pinkish fluid running out from under the radiator. "Hey, look, Dad, at the stuff coming out of that radiator." Dad is straining forward, watching the light. He does not want to be an armchair diagnostic mechanic. "Mmm," he says, tersely. "Let's go, let's *go*," he mutters at the light. We start up. "Hey, mister," Peter says out the window, "your pink lemonade is bubbling out of your car." We all laugh. "Mister" does not appear to have heard. We are on our way.

Vacations are one of the compensations for the long and irregular hours involved in being a minister. Most churches offer their minister a month's vacation—thirty-one days, with four or five Sundays, depending on how the days of the particular month fall. We have known ministers who do not take a vacation. One such minister is said to have remarked, in explaining why he stayed on duty throughout the year, "The devil doesn't take a vacation," to which one of his hearers replied, "Maybe that's why he's the devil."

We do take our vacation—usually all of it in the summertime, though Hoyt has sometimes saved a few days for some optional meeting later in the year, or as an extra getaway after Easter.

Sometimes we split up the vacation, taking a couple of weeks at a time, with a week back at the church and at home for catching up with pastoral work and getting the clothes clean again.

For families who live on the limited income of a minister's salary, a month's vacation can tax the ingenuity for ways to use the time. Vacations at home just do not work for ministers— occasions arise that call for the minister's presence or judgment, and neither he nor his parishioners can resist involving him in these occasions. People call up, extra office work is all too pressing, and the vacation spirit is just not present. But most ministers cannot afford, either, to take month-long vacations at resorts or to travel for a month with attendant motel and restaurant expenses.

Many ministers' families, along with half the rest of the country, go camping, with anything from tents and sleeping bags to fancy trailers. But we do not camp, at least not so far. Neither of us is that enamored of roughing it, or that handy with hatchet and tent poles, to make tent camping an inviting option. And the prospect of pulling a trailer along behind us seems too nerve-wracking to contemplate happily, let alone the overdose of togetherness involved in sleeping six people in a one-room trailer for a month's time (and a more elaborate trailer is no economy).

Many families of ministers have bought or built a summer home, to which they go for vacations now and which they may plan to extend into year-round living quarters at the time they retire. A summer home gives to the children in the family some continuing roots over the years of moving into and out of church parsonages, some place to look back upon with continuing associations, to be "a place of our own" in a sense in which a succession of parsonages can never be. Knowing what it means to me

to be able to go back home to the place of my childhood, to remember when the large maple trees were saplings, to have a
childhood full of associations—the smell of honeysuckle on the
front porch or the way the sun streams through the dining-room
windows in early morning, of stairways and fireplaces and
pulleyed clotheslines—I regret that my children will not have
this kind of rich and continuing fabric as a backdrop to their
childhood. But they will not, except as they may have it in the
homes of their grandparents, to which they have returned
through all the years of their lives. Part of the ritual of going
home to these places is to rush around to the best-known spots:
the drawer and the closet where the children's toys are kept; the
walk among the cluster of bushes and small trees that edge the
lot—an area that seemed like a giant woods when first the children started walking here; the attic stairs that come down out
of the ceiling; the particular quality of the sandy dirt under the
back porch, where a couple of years ago Stephen discovered some
ant lions, a species of life that must have existed there for forty
years, unsung, unhonored, and undug, until he came along to
count it among his year's most important finds. To go "home"
to the place that was home to me gives to Mary a confirmation
of a past she is eager to know about. "Tell me what it was like
when you were a little girl—how were your dresses, what was
your hair fixed like, what kind of shoes did you have?" Feminine
question, these, and, in a family in which we ladies are outnum-
bered two to one, a peculiar delight to us. Mary seems to have
found a special security for herself in the home that was mine
for so many years: it is not only the people there she loves, but
the house itself. "It's so *cozy,*" she says, and lingers on the word.
She speaks of the yellow roses on the wallpaper in the bedroom

that was mine, and she says, coming home in the car after we have all been together, and indicating a stone she is turning slowly in her hand, "I'm going to keep it, for a remembrance."

On our vacations, we visit family, scattered as our families are over the eastern and middlewestern United States, a vacation habit which recalls that couplet:

> People who plan inexpensive vacations
> Usually plan them around their relations.

We are fortunate in that we like each other's relatives—at least the going folklore about family relationships would make us think we are blest beyond the common expectations in this regard. Of course each family has its share of "characters," but they help make life interesting.

We always have a visit with each set of parents—sometimes at their homes, sometimes at a vacation spot of mutual liking. Sometimes the family of a brother or sister will join us. Sometimes everyone in the family will be there, at some place big enough to hold us all. We swim and read and rest and play games together and lie in the sun. But mainly, we talk—sisters with sisters, brothers with sisters and with each other, in-laws together, aunts and uncles with nieces and nephews, parents and children, talking. Cousins become reacquainted, new babies are introduced, old occasions are recalled, old jokes are laughed at again and new ones are passed around— all the rituals of love and relationship by which we learn again and savor together the stream of life we share, and reaffirm for ourselves the mystery and fact of who we are.

One year we drove out to the middle west, to a city where Hoyt has a large settlement of relatives, and where as a child he had gone back "home" with his father and to the community not far away which was "home" to his mother, though none of her family lives there now. In this city, in addition to an assortment of aunts, uncles, and cousins, lives Hoyt's grandmother, a woman over ninety years old, who carries her years with a wisdom, zest, and merriment that is worth traveling a thousand miles to see. Hoyt wanted the children to know their great-grandmother better, as he had known her mother, his great-grandmother, when he was a boy—to know that one can both revere and enjoy those who achieve long age, and that, in this time of the glorification of youth, a face deeply lined with wrinkles and a body of slow and careful gait can make the heart leap with recognition and love.

Hoyt is not one to let a sightseeing opportunity pass. On one of our return trips from a vacation we were to come close to a natural phenomenon known as the ice mine. Hoyt, interested as he is in all unusual occurrences and eager to share this enthusiasm, thought the children should not miss seeing it. I had already seen the ice mine, having been taken there by Hoyt on a similar side excursion years before, and I wasn't sure it was worth the necessary admission fee and time, but back we went.

The ice mine is a formation of ice, visible through a hole in the ground. Around this hole a small building has been erected, so that admission to view the ice can be charged. The ice in the mine is reputed to be there in summer and to disappear in winter, though I doubt that many people go to check about it in winter —snow covering the ground and all that. There are various theories about the ice: that it is a relic of a glacier, that it is due to some chemical reaction of underground elements, or that cold air in winter is driven deep into the ground and, with the rising heat of summer air, slowly emerges, forming ice as it passes through the earth's surface. The theories are more impressive than the mine.

The path to the ice mine was woodsy and green, and lovely flowers grew along it. The woods were cool with a welcome coolness on a hot day. The inevitable souvenir shop was more tasteful than most, and the bottles of soft drinks were bought and consumed.

Hoyt paid our admission fees and we stood outside the door of the small shed covering the opening to the ice mine. We were admitted to the viewing chamber. It was as I had remembered: a wooden platform was built around a hole in the ground, with a guard rail around the hole to prevent some eager tourist from tumbling in. Down through the hole one could see a stream of grayish white granular material—the ice! Against the rail the awestruck tourists pressed while we heard the measured intonations of the guide, describing the mine. I had remembered that there were colored lights playing on the ice. This time—no lights. The ice did look slushy. Perhaps the lights were too hot for this season's crop.

Peter was standing beside me. "Is this it?" he whispered. The other children were nudging each other and whispering words I did not hear and, I hope, neither did the guide. When we got outside and back in the car John said, solemnly, "It was an unforgettable experience. I have been profoundly affected."

On another occasion, on the way home from a vacation week, we took time to look for a particular lakeside spot at which Hoyt had spent two months with his family, the summer that he was thirteen. Since John was thirteen, and we were driving through the Lake Champlain country, Hoyt wanted to find the place.

He and I had looked for it once before, on a week-end trip the spring after we were married. I had heard the family stories— about how Dad had taken the late train to the city each Sunday night, how Mother had had to park the car in the common parking area and walk the long walk in to their cottage, very late at night, with the ever-present danger of skunks. The time we had looked before had been off season. There had been snow on the ground and the roadway had been closed up, inaccessible.

But the wish to go back is with Hoyt still and now, fifteen years later, we are looking again. We drive along the road, as close as we can get to the eastern shore of Lake Champlain. We take the road toward Douglass—he thinks that is the right way, though the town itself has changed.

"Yes, I remember this main street," he says, as we drive through it and then out into the country. "Now, let me see, I think it is down this way." He turns right. His sense of direction is infallible. "There, I think we go along this road." We drive on for about half a mile. "Now, it should be about here that the road goes down." We come to the remnants of an old stone fence, crumbling into a weed-choked trail that looks as though it might have been a road.

"I wonder," he says. "I think maybe this is the road." But there is a slanting wooden stile across it now, and the vestiges of road are barely visible through tall grass and bushes and untrodden vines. We can see only that once there must have been a road here.

"Oh . . ." he says, and his voice trails off, "I guess that was it." It was, after all, twenty-five years ago that he was here with his family, and fifteen since he and I had been here together. "Well—" he says, tentatively, and drives slowly on. We are quiet.

The moment speaks for itself. After a few minutes he says, "The only way we could get there—we could go down toward Douglass and rent a boat. We could *ride* over there. I know I could find it from the water—it's right along the edge of the lake, and there's a kind of double bay. It's right opposite the Four Brothers Islands. You can see them from here." He points to four islands, lying close together offshore. He is still musing. "We could rent a boat. . . ."

We have been boating all week and are eager to move along. One of the children says, "Do we have to?" but softly, because it does matter to him, and they know it.

"It's important to Daddy," I say. "We can at least go and see about a boat."

A little farther along the road, as we are heading tentatively toward Douglass, we come upon another road, turning back toward the shore.

"Wait a minute!" he says. "I think *this* may be the road." His voice leaps in his throat. "Yes," he says, turning, "this is the road. It isn't overgrown after all." There. He is reprieved. He is not awaking in a land grown old. The road is preserved, and trafficked, and viable, and so is his childhood, and so is he.

We drive along and pass a number of small roads leading in to homes and camps along the lake shore. It is a Sunday morning, and the shore is quiet. But then a trio of children run out along the edge of the woods. They seem an anachronism. This is a thirty-year-old land and the children seem out of place, startling, here. We read each sign carefully, looking for the old name. "Probably," he says, having been burned once, "the place isn't there anymore. Probably they sold it to someone else, or maybe it's been abandoned. It was pretty primitive, and I suppose it would have cost too much to modernize it." He has told us the camp had no electricity and they used kerosene lamps.

But ahead of us is a sign, a tan slab of wood with trim green lettering, in good taste and condition; it marks the end of a well-kept road leading toward the shore. "There!" he says. "There it is!" and we all laugh with relief and happiness. For he is affirmed again.

He turns the car in and we start down the road. The sign has said Members Only, but we can explain, if anyone asks. He is remembering it all now. "There are the old garages," he says, "where we used to put the cars," and, "These buildings have changed." We drive around a bit and park the car, and he sets out and we follow. These are deep woods, and cool, and shafts of sunlight slant through tree branches and illuminate a single bed of moss or a small stand of fern. The morning cobwebs are still wet, and the sunlight reveals them, concentric filigrees of light. We walk quietly, in single file because the paths are narrow and we are, in a way, intruders here.

"The cottage we stayed in was back here," he says, "the last one out."

A man looks up from a porch, his newspaper in his hand. "Good morning," he says.

"Good morning," Hoyt says, and nods.

"And isn't it a lovely one," says the man, and goes back to reading his paper. We cross the small ravine, and Stephen pauses by the tiny stream and then catches up with us. We have reached the shore of the lake. A few boats are moored there. A handsome house sits on the point between the two inlets. "That was the Lewis house," he says. "They had a cabin cruiser they kept here.

And we kept our rowboat we rented for the summer moored along that beach. Once we rowed out to the Four Brothers."

"That must have been a long row," I say. "It looks like a long way out."

"It was," he says, and smiles, remembering. "Mother got a little anxious about it because a storm started to blow up before we got back." I shudder to think of it.

"Let me take your picture," I say. The children line up with him, the lake behind them. "There—" it is done, and we walk on. There is a peace to this place, compounded by the quiet beauty of the morning and the cool green air and the treasure of this piece of his youth we have found. We walk on farther. The children are acquiescent, but they do not care that much that we rediscover each spot for him. But he cares, and so do I —for him, and for me because it was his.

"There," he says, as we pass a thick patch of spruce. "I don't remember whether that is the same cottage, improved, that we had, or whether it's a different one. But that's the place, at the edge of the grounds. That's where our cottage was." We stop at some distance, because he doesn't want to be conspicuous to the people who live there now, or to intrude, even, that much into the present. He doesn't want them to know why we came. We see a porch along one side, and there is a playpen there and a baby in it, walking around the edge of the playpen and chewing on a toy. "We had a porch there, too," he says, "if that *is* the same house."

We must be on our way. We go back to the car and get in. "Thank you," he says, turning to the children, "for bearing with me on my sentimental journey." They are quiet, their usual jocularity hushed for a moment at least.

We drive out the road, and on the way we pass a car coming in. The driver is alone and he is wearing a clergyman's collar. "Maybe he's coming back after conducting an early service in town," I say.

"Maybe," he says. "It's about that time."

X
Gold and Myrrth and
Don't Be Incensed

Gifts to the minister and his family are among the delightful imponderables of parsonage life. They are, for the most part, offered from a generous heart and with only an occasional lack of judgment—like the gift of a twelve-pound ham to the newly married couple who were not yet in possession of a refrigerator. While, in contrast to former days, gifts, particularly of food, are not usually a major item in the minister's family economy, ministers are still receivers of gifts, and it is helpful if the minister and his family are able to accept gifts with the warmth and delight with which most of them are offered.

There is a whole psychology of gifts, and the hazards of giving and receiving gifts by persons in public life have been much discussed of late. There are people who think that giving gifts to the minister is bad business—that the minister will be tempted to compromise his message in deference to those who give him gifts. But, all the cries of paternalism and antiprofessionalism notwithstanding, and while care is needed, of course, the urge to give something to the minister and the ability to receive it with genuine gratitude are still symbols of the love in which the minister and his family at least hope to be held by the members of a congregational family. Certainly we do not, in this or any other relationship, "own" those whom we love. And even gifts offered out of a sense of guilt can be agents of pleasure and grace.

We have received gifts without number, and for most of these we have been truly grateful. Many have been gifts from individuals who seem to include the minister's family almost as an extension of their own, and they bring to us some sample of their work: jars of homemade pickles, spicy and crisp; nationality pastries, painstakingly and beautifully made; jars of fresh fruit, cut and awash in their own juice to refresh a Christmas supper. There have been gifts to celebrate the births of our children, flowers to express sympathy for our sorrows, gifts of gratitude— an antique plate cherished for most of a lifetime and given to Hoyt by an elderly shut-in lady of little means, because she wants to somehow say "thank you" in more than words for calls he has made in gladness and compassion. Some gifts are examples of a hobby shared: a painting, a hand-wrought bracelet, a lovely rag rug, some choice fruit from a garden.

There have been gifts of service and time, countless hours of work given in painting, building, designing, repairing, on parsonage projects. These are gifts to the church, of course, but they are gifts from which we, the family, have got the benefit.

Other gifts to the minister and his family come from groups in the church or from the congregation as a whole. There is a certain delicate comedy involved in some of these gifts: a Sunday school class at its monthly business meeting brings up under "new business" the matter of a Christmas gift to the pastor, and all kinds of currents of approval and disapproval, of economic

and social appraisal, are set loose to swirl, for the most part un-
spoken, around the motion before the group. Or a gift of money
is to be collected as a congregational gift to the pastor and of
course he must not see it happening, though he can hardly be
unsuspecting of the meaning of the sudden silence when he
comes into a classroom on a Sunday morning in mid-December.

For these and for other reasons, congregational gifts to the minister are less common seasonal events in larger city churches than
they are in smaller, more rurally oriented churches, where gifts
of one kind or another have been part of the traditional method
by which ministers have been paid. It is a little hard for the minister who receives a gift from his congregation at Christmastime,
particularly if it is a gift of cash, not to measure the success of
his personal relationships by the relative size of the gift: if they
collected more money for our Christmas present last year than
this, does that mean they don't like me as well this year? Because
they gave me more money my first year here does that mean they
are becoming disenchanted? Am I doing something wrong? Is
it time I moved? All kinds of unhelpful speculations can start
in the minister's mind, and perhaps in the congregation's, too.
Whereas in fact the real success of a man's ministry—the extent
to which he is able to bring to his people the reality of God's love
and righteousness—may at any moment have little to do with his
popularity or the extent to which people on a random Sunday
morning feel like kicking in a little something extra for his
Christmas present.

It can also be ironically observed by the minister and his family
that churches, like individuals, sometimes give lavish gifts out of
a sense of guilt. I think of the church from which we received
a television set as a *welcoming* gift, a piece of extravagant gener-

osity that became a bit more plausible when we realized, after living in the community a litte longer, how much mischief was afoot. We were delighted with the television set. We had not had one at all before, and our small son was reacting to our refusal to capitulate to the television culture by spending the maximum time allowed at the neighbors, standing on their front porch so he could hear me if I called, with his nose pressed against the door screen, the better to see the television in the living room. I had been wondering why he kept coming home with a smudge on the end of his nose, until the neighbor mother asked me if I wouldn't please let him come into their house to watch television —he was making a nose-height depression in the door screen, and she was sure he must be straining his eyes!

Not only the television set was given us while we were there, but, after the mischief surfaced and as seasonal occasions afforded, other lavish gifts, and these gifts became a measure of the support of those in the church who were "for" the minister, a kind of reassurance offered in defiance of those who were not. I doubt whether these gifts were discussed or even thought of in these terms by either side of the petty warfare, much less by the rest of the people, who thought church was a place to which one came to worship God rather than to play out his community hostilities. But knowing something of how wondrously mixed are our own motives in much that we do, we know that for others, too, all is not what it seems. And far from this being a disillusioning thought, it serves to remind us of how thoroughly bound up with the pressures and drives of our everyday life is our understanding of God, of how this permeates every facet of human life.

Among the tenderest gifts which are given to a minister and

his family are those given on the occasion of his departure from
a church. Sometimes these have been, for us, gifts from individuals—a milk-glass compote that has become part of our traditional Christmastime table decoration, a pair of pillowcases with
inserts of fine tatting, a handsome carving set, a pair of vases.

Sometimes a group in the church will make a special farewell
gift to the minister. One of our choicest items is a blue and white
quilt, given to us by the ladies of a particular Sunday school class
on the occasion of our departure from our first church. The
ladies had designed and made the quilt themselves, with the
names of members of the church embroidered along spokes of
the wheels that constitute the pattern of the quilt. This project
was not only a tender expression of farewell to us but a means of
raising money—for the inclusion of each name on the quilt, the
ladies charged a nominal sum, thus swelling their class treasury.
This combination of motives might be considered indelicate, but
only to an outsider. For us, the ladies' open espousal of their dual
intention added charm to the project, then and now.

At the occasion of farewell, in large churches and in small,
there is usually a congregational reception for the departing minister and his family, and at this time a farewell gift from the congregation is presented. (I have heard of receptions which, for
economy of time, labor, and sentimentality, were at the same time
a farewell for the departing minister and a welcome to the new
minister. I do not see how these can avoid being occasions of
strain, and I hope I never have to be part of the honored crowd
at such a gathering.) Gifts to the minister and his family at farewell receptions depend of course on many circumstances, such
as the length of the minister's service in that church and the size
and affluence of the congregation. Silver and china are often

given, or a gift of money to be spent on something of the minister's choosing. A certain amount of comparative jocularity goes on among clergy families as they discuss the generous farewell gifts from former churches, who "really made it worthwhile for us to leave."

Among large churches it is increasingly common to give the minister, sometime during his tenure with the church, the handsome gift of a trip abroad, usually to the Holy Land. The assumption is that a man's faith and ministry will be strengthened by visiting the sites of Jesus' life and ministry, whereas, to quote a world traveler's remark on the subject of visiting the Holy Land, "A man of strong faith can survive it." Perhaps, however, it is a good thing for a minister to test his faith against the commercialism and crowding that have taken place over the Garden of Gethsemane and the rival sites for other important Christian events. World travel is, for most people, an experience of growth, and if the minister's heart really lies in refreshing his life, and therefore his faith, by visiting the fjords of Norway, maybe he can work it in on the way home.

There is another group of gifts offered to the minister that can indeed be a major factor in his family's economy, which are offered out of regard to his profession and in recognition of the fact that, especially in earlier days, ministers were poorly paid. These are gifts of discounts from stores and of discounted, or ocassionally free, medical service. We feel about store discounts to ministers as we do about trading stamps: we do not believe in them (there is no reason why a department store should support the clergy, whose maintenance should be the responsibility of their particular parishes), but when clergy discounts, like trading stamps, are routinely given as part of store policy, we accept them.

The matter of special consideration in medical fees can be a much more important economic factor than a ten per cent discount in a department store. We would not choose a doctor because he was known to be generous with ministers—health is much too important for that—and we have cheerfully paid for the full value of medical service, grateful that it was available and that we were *able* to pay for it. On the other hand, knowing how expensive good health care can be and how we will not do without it, we would be less than honest, and certainly ungracious, to pretend that when this gift is offered it is anything but welcome.

Most gifts to the minister and his family are gifts of love and regard or are given out of respect to his profession. A few are symbols of how the battle lines form. There are other gifts, and these may also be gifts of love and regard, that are given to the minister and his family as to someone to whom it is legitimate to give things one doesn't know what else to do with, but which one can't in good conscience throw away. These gifts are fun to receive; they are often useful, they sometimes have hilarious overtones, and, if one understands them, they carry a minimum of responsibility. The appropriate mood in which to receive them runs something like this: If the giver can't use it, you don't need to feel too duty-bound to use it either, though get from it what good you can.

I think of the vat of chicken gravy we were given by the cooks after one church supper. Do not misunderstand me—we love to get leftover food from church suppers: it is usually delicious, it is already prepared, and it is free. But there was this vat of chicken gravy. The chicken had been eaten, and there must have been about eight quarts of gravy left, and what to do with it? There was no Salvation Army center, no children's home, nothing of that kind in town to which it could be given. Maybe the minister could use it. The cooks asked him. He was sure we could use it, he being as compulsive as anyone else about not wasting food, and not wanting to hurt the ladies' feelings by turning down their offer. So he brought it home, in a huge steel tub.

Eight quarts of chicken gravy would not faze me now, because we have a freezer. Now I would dutifully put it in containers and save it, for perhaps two or three years, reheating and using a box or two of it from time to time, until I realized that we'd never finish it up, either. But at that time we didn't have a freezer—only the small freezer section at the bottom of the refrigerator, and we couldn't give it all over to the chicken gravy. When Hoyt brought it home I thought—all that? For just six of us? It was delicious gravy, and we did our best. We had it on toast for lunch. I used it as a base for soup. I served it as a sauce on broccoli. But after about three days we had had enough, and with only slightly guilty feelings we threw the rest away, pouring it ceremonially down the drain while we all stood around and watched.

Or there was the incident of the rabbits. A young man in our church (I suppose he was about fifteen and it told something about the churchiness of his upbringing that at this relatively young age he thought of the minister as the recipient of his generosity) called us up one day just as we were about to go for a family ride. Hoyt answered the telephone. The young man said he had been hunting and had shot a couple of rabbits. His parents were out of town, and anyway they didn't care for rabbit, and he was staying by himself for a couple of days and he wondered if *we'd* like the rabbits. He had already cleaned them, and if Hoyt would come and get them, this fellow would be glad to give them to us.

Hoyt, ever eager for new gustatory experiences, said yes, we would like the rabbits. "Sure we would. Thank you. Sure. . . . I'll be right up." He concluded the conversation, told me what was up, and went off to get the rabbits. Never having eaten rabbit, I was a little skeptical, but willing to try. After all, look at the French, for whom rabbit has been a staple, and everyone knows what good taste in food the French have.

When Hoyt came back with the rabbits, I was upstairs putting the baby into her sweater set. He called up the stairs, "Shall I put them in the refrigerator?" I shouted back yes, and we all left for our ride.

In the car Hoyt told me, gently, that the rabbits, though they were cleaned (euphemism for eviscerated), were not skinned. Not skinned! Visions of the furry corpses reclining in the refrigerator came to mind. And here we'd never even eaten rabbit, let alone do a take-apart job first. I remembered my college physiology lab where the professor had tried to get past our squeamishness quickly by dissecting a cat during the first lab period.

We came home from the ride, and I got the dinner and tried not to notice the rabbits until later. Peter, who was four at the time and had heard us talking in the car about the gift, opened the refrigerator door, looked inside, and said, "*I* ain't eating any of them dead bunnies."

After dinner we tackled the rabbits. Hoyt, feeling somewhat responsible for having brought on the predicament, offered to help me. We got out the cooking encyclopedia and found instructions for "dressing" rabbit (a piece of nomenclature which has always impressed me as singularly inappropriate), including a graphic paragraph on "removal of fur." One of the precautions was to use rubber gloves, to avoid the possibility of contracting tularemia, a widespread disease that can be transmitted to humans through the improper handling of uncooked rabbit. We had one pair of rubber gloves. We agreed that I could probably handle the process better than Hoyt could. Neither of us is any surgeon, but I do paint, sew, give haircuts, and otherwise evidence dexterity. Besides, the work area was the kitchen and the subject, eventually, food, and that was my domain. So I put on the gloves and Hoyt read me the instructions and otherwise lent support to the project. The possibility of ever eating the material at hand became more unappealing by the minute, but it had become a matter of moral courage and we couldn't stop now.

According to the book the person skinning the rabbit should be able to remove the fur-bearing skin all in one piece. It didn't seem to work that way, particularly with the first rabbit. By the time we got to the second rabbit things went much better. Finally, after much cutting, tearing, sighing, running commentary, and turning off and on of the faucet, we finished skinning and cutting up the rabbits. Then we put them, enshrouded in many layers of aluminum foil, into the freezing section of our refrigerator, and there we left them for six weeks, letting time do its healing work. Then we ate them, enshrouded with sauce. The taste of the sauce rather overpowered the taste of the rabbit, which was fine with me. I wasn't too hungry anyway.

But one of my favorite impromptu gifts was the gift of mentioned unmentionables. In one of our churches there was a lady of mature years who supplemented her income by selling a line of underwear, selected and purchased through catalogues. We knew each other well, and one day she approached me a bit apologetically and said there was something she wanted to ask me. I said what was that and she said well, she had ordered a pair of white underpants for a gift for her niece and somehow the underpants had slipped out of their protective wrapper and fallen on the floor of the car and had got a little dusty. I nodded sympathetically. Well, she had washed the underpants, and they were as good as new, but she didn't really want to give them as a gift. Now she thought, she said, eyeing me with a guarded appraisal, that the niece was probably the same size as I was, and she wondered if I would mind—well, she didn't like to throw them away, and of course she couldn't send them back—would I mind if she gave me the underpants? I assured her that I would be delighted—as, indeed, I would—to receive the underpants, though I would be glad to buy them from her, as who can have too many? No, no, she wanted to give them to me, if I was sure I wouldn't mind. Indeed, I wouldn't mind, I would be delighted to have them, and it was very good of her to pass them along to me. Well, she said, she would bring them to church next Sunday and give them to me then.

By next Sunday I had forgotten that this was the day on which I was to receive the underpants, but I went to church of course and sat a couple of rows farther back than usual, as some of the local college students were in my accustomed place. At the end of the service I went back, as I always did, to stand near one of the doors to greet some of the people as they left. Among the last to leave was my friend, looking a little chagrined and carrying a small flattened package in her hand. She gave me the package and said, in a jovial Sunday morning voice but with a touch of consternation, "I put the pants on the seat where you sit, but the college boys came in and sat on them."

"Thank you!" I said, my pleasure in the gift infused by the image of the unsuspecting college boys being held under anxious surveillance during the entire worship service while they rose and reseated themselves—on? or off?—the package intended for me.

XI
Living with the Rules

I first heard of the *Discipline of the Methodist Church* in a series of offhand references Hoyt made in conversations with other Methodists about the workings of the Church. I assumed that the *Discipline* must be something like the Episcopal *Book of Common Prayer,* or a Catholic missal—some standard service book, probably dating from John Wesley's time, which churches put in their hymn racks along with the hymnals and you hoped that when the organ started a hymn introduction you picked up the right book first. Or that possibly the *Discipline* might be a kind of Wesleyan version of Calvin's *Institutes*—some systematic exposition of Methodist belief and rules for church operation.

Before Hoyt and I were married, when we went to church together it was likely to be to a Baptist church. Since I had grown up as a Baptist and would surely become a Methodist in due time, Hoyt considered our attendance at Baptist churches a good trade: he would go to a Baptist church with me for maybe a year or two, and for the rest of our life I would go to a Methodist church with him. During the first couple of years of our marriage we lived in a New England university community where the non-denominational seminary Hoyt attended was located, and more often than not we attended the University Chapel services—which perpetuated my blissful ignorance of the Methodist *Discipline* for a year or so longer. I was, at any rate, much more concerned with the theological and social questions that were stirring the seminary community, and with how I was going to play out my life as a minister's wife, than I was with the particular patterns of the Methodist Church, with which I knew I would become familiar as occasion demanded.

The first startling fact about the *Discipline* that emerged for me was the fact that, far from being a constant historic document dating back from the days of John Wesley, the whole thing was reissued every four years! This is, in a way, a minor refraction in the image one has of a book, and yet it was jarring to me. The *Discipline* looked so much like a "permanent" book: it had practically the page format and the heft of a Bible—dark hard covers, gold-letter stamping on the spine of the book, more than eight hundred pages. And how expensive it must be to get out a book like this so frequently; think of all the C.A.R.E. packages we could send with the money that must be spent on printing and buying a new version every four years. Here I was not even a Methodist yet, and I had had enough of the *Discipline* already.

A much more important encounter with the *Discipline* came when Hoyt was preparing, during his third year at seminary, for full ordination as a minister in the Methodist Church, and he described to me the dilemma posed for him by the "Wesley Questions." With this description began my real education on the subject of the Methodist *Discipline*.

The Wesley Questions are a set of nineteen questions that were formulated by John Wesley; they are contained in the *Discipline,* and they are asked of every minister before he is fully ordained into the Methodist Church. They include many questions to which one could happily answer with the expected "Yes": "Have you faith in Christ?" "Have you studied the doctrines of the Methodist Church?" "Will you visit from house to house?" Who can quarrel with these? There are others for which the possibilities of interpretation are so wide they, too, do not cause serious trouble. "Are you in debt so as to embarrass you in your work?" probably tells more about the candidate's threshold of embarrassment than about the state of his finances; candidates for the ministry, many of whom have had to take out loans to complete their education, have a good go-around about the meaning of that question but can usually manage to answer with the expected "No." Even the directions, "Never trifle away time; neither spend any more time at any one place than is strictly necessary. . . . Do everything exactly at the time," are recognized to say as much about John Wesley's frenetic compulsions as about the pursuit of the ministry and can be accepted in the understanding that time spent in leisure is not really time "trifled away."

But the really stunning items in the Wesley Questions are enough to make a religiously sophisticated man blanch: "Are you going on to perfection?" and "Do you expect to be made perfect in love in this life?" How was Hoyt going to answer *these* questions in the holy service, before the assembled multitude? Not only did I sympathize with Hoyt's realism about the possibilities of even the most dedicated clergyman being "made perfect in love in this life" but I had had a couple of grim encounters with people who believed they had already achieved such a state of perfection, and I surely would have hated to be married to one of them.

The Bishop of our Conference made a visit to the seminary campus that spring, to interview the men who were coming up for ordination, and Hoyt shared with the Bishop his feeling that he was not going to be able to answer the Wesley Questions in the way in which they were intended to be answered. The Bishop, on inquiring, found that Hoyt was no more of a heretic than he himself was and asked Hoyt what he felt *would* be palatable answers to give to the troublesome few. Well, he would have to qualify some of them. In answer to the question on whether he would keep the General Rules of the Church, with some of whose prejudices Hoyt could not agree, he would have to say, "In general, yes." In answer to the question about "being made perfect in love" he could answer, "I hope so." (Who can blame a man for hoping?) In answer to the question on recommending "fasting or abstinence, both by precept and example," Hoyt, having a healthy appetite and seeing no merit, per se, in depriving his slightly underweight frame, would answer, "When advisable." These slight deviations from the expected answers meeting both the Bishop's standards of appropriate conforming to the spirit of the Church and Hoyt's need to preserve his integrity, they agreed he should go ahead and give these answers, and if the congregation at the service was confused by a slightly garbled lack of unanimity in the response of the candidates to the famous Wesley Questions—well, that would just add more mystery to the service; which it did, as someone in attendance later asked Hoyt what he was proclaiming over there that was different from what the other men were saying.

We have since talked with other ministers who have had their own versions of "what to do about the Wesley Questions," including one man whose Bishop had the custom of asking candidates for ordination these questions in private session and then reporting to the Conference that the man had indeed been able to answer them. Our friend approached his interview with some misgiving, and when the Bishop asked him, in summary form, "Have you read the questions?" and then, "Can you answer them?" he answered "Yes" to the first and started on a "Yes, but—" to the second, only to have the Bishop cut him off with a "That's all right" before he launched into his protests and then report back to the assembled Conference body that yes, this particular candidate had been "able to answer the questions."

Another friend reports that when he answered, "I hope so," to the question, "Do you expect to be made perfect in love in this life?" the Bishop to whom he was speaking, evidently somewhat taken aback, had given him a quizzical look and then had said, "I hope so, too."

The General Rules, to which a summary acquiescence is asked of ministerial candidates in the course of the above-described Wesley Questions, apply not only to ministers of the Methodist Church but to all members of the Church as well, including, of course, ministers' wives, most of whom are a law-abiding lot. (Unless the minister, like Hosea of old, has married his wife to reform her—which, while it was a wonderful metaphor for illustrating the love of God, didn't work out too well as a marriage.) The General Rules cover a multitude of sins, both of action and of attitude, and were some ecclesiastical hatchet man to try to enforce them and to separate from the churches all who transgressed any of these rules, there would be no one left, either in the congregation or in the pulpit. They are, however, useful, not only as sometimes-relevant standards of conduct but also as quaint indications of what were regarded as qualities of grace in past times, and for inveighing against some person or doctrine that rubs us the wrong way: there is always some one of the General Rules that can be invoked as evidence or held up to ridicule, depending on which side of the bar we stand on.

The unequivocal sections of the Rules include advice against inferior language or taste; various rules against specific civil and moral offenses, such as stealing, smuggling, or borrowing without intending to repay; exhortations to attend public and private worship; paraphrases of various Biblical admonitions about doing good to all men; and, in an italicized adverb, a charming warning not to take our likelihood of being ill-regarded by the world as a license for unsavory whooping it up ("looking that men should say all manner of evil . . . *falsely,* for the Lord's sake").

Among the provisions which by common consent we no longer consider relevant are those against the wearing of gold and against slaveholding; wedding rings are an accepted part of the mystique of even the pious, and while we can scarcely congratulate ourselves on the church's role in matters of race, at least the steam that swirled around the issue of slavery now hovers over more contemporary aspects of race discrimination. The rules that we are expected to employ Methodists in preference to non-Methodists, to buy from each other, and to help each other in business come from a time when the economic success of a businessman was perhaps jeopardized by his espousing the far-out sect of Methodist Societies. Discriminatory employment based on religion is now in many places illegal and certainly in ill repute, and we are so far removed from economic discrimination that in one of our major cities a huge department store sits on property owned by a local Methodist church, which receives handsome rental payments for its use. We can scarcely ask for special patronage from one another on the grounds that we are excluded from the Establishment.

A particularly convenient handle on which to hang all sorts of red flags has been that portion of the *Discipline* which dealt with alcoholic beverages. Upon the whetstone of this group of admonitions, everyone could grind his ax. Those who thought the Church should take a stronger stand on the matter of alcohol pointed out that the General Rules not only decried buying, selling, or drinking "spirituous liquors" but that the *Discipline* listed all kinds of further involvement condoning beverage alcohol as reasons why a church member might be brought to trial —for renting his property for the manufacture or sale of beverage alcohol, even for co-signing a bond for any person engaged in "such traffic." Those who, on the other hand, wished to free themselves or others from being morally bound by these strictures either attempted to put them in the "outdated" category or heaped scorn upon the hypocrisy of our pretending to take the *Discipline* seriously on this matter at all: why, the *Discipline* called for "total abstinence from alcoholic beverages" as a particular qualification for membership on the Official Board, and how many of our Official Boards could qualify as auxiliaries to the W.C.T.U.? Or, if those who oppose the rules on beverage alcohol were advocates of sweet reason, they used semantic analysis rather than blistering scorn. They pointed out that the wording of the *Discipline* was not that the Official Board must abstain from alcohol but that it was "expected" that they do so.

For church members, the ruling was qualified by the phrase, "unless in cases of extreme necessity," and everyone had to interpret for himself the fore and aft limits of his own "extreme necessity." Maybe social pressure creates necessity for one person but not for another or, to put it another way, Is one man's Coke another man's Scotch and soda?

In one of the communities where Hoyt was minister, he learned soon after his arrival in town that several members of the church were bartenders, which is a bit unusual as a vocation for a Methodist. (Not for a Lutheran, or an Episcopalian, among Protestants, but for a Methodist.) During the course of Hoyt's ministry there he had occasion to take in as a new member a man who owned and served at another one of the local bars. In conversation with one of the leaders of the church the matter of the new member's vocation came up, and the layman wondered, in a mood of genuine puzzlement, what the attitude of the church should be to such persons in view of the strictures of the Methodist *Discipline.* Legally, did not such a vocation for a Methodist carry with it the threat of a church trial and possible exclusion? Hoyt pointed out that while the *Discipline* did indeed say that such a person "may" be tried, it did not say he must, and that also according to the *Discipline* and equally offensive as a cause for which a person might be tried were "sinful tempers and words" and "uncharitable or unprofitable conversation," and, on that basis, who was going to cast the first stone?

But our stereotypes about the church and alcohol persist. In this same community Hoyt wished to pay a pastoral call on one of the bartending members and, on learning that the man spent most of his waking hours at his place of business, went to see him at his bar during the unbusy hours of afternoon. Not only

did word of the Methodist minister's visit travel speedily around
the town but it was sufficiently surprising to the man himself
that at the door of church the following Sunday he said, about
his unaccustomed appearance at morning worship, "I figured if
you could come to see me at my place, I could come to see you
at yours." And weeks later at a ministers' meeting in a distant
city, a minister from many miles away paid Hoyt the compli-
ment of saying, "I heard that some Methodist minister up your
way went to call on one of his parishioners in a bar. I figured it
might be you."

Times do sometimes change for the better. In 1968, at the historic General Conference at which the Methodist Church and
the Evangelical United Brethren Church joined to form the
United Methodist Church, in addition to taking far more important action in regard to national and world problems, the
Church straightened its own house and amended its rules on alcohol to *recommend* abstinence but to leave the decision to the
conscience of each individual.

What else was there in the *Discipline,* besides alcohol rules,
Wesley Questions, and General Rules? There were descriptions
of the organizations of the Church (enough to encourage, at
least temporarily, the yen for anarchy of any ex-Baptist). There
were the orders of worship for the Church, the decisions of the
Judicial Council—the Supreme Court of the Methodist Church
—and descriptions of the duties and activities of all the Church
boards. There was a long section on Pensions and Permanent
Funds, including such enigmatic listings in the Table of Contents
as "Joint Contributory Annuity Fund" and "Death Benefit Program," which latter phrase was, I suppose, the Church's attempt
to come to grips with the unrealistic euphemism of the term

"life insurance" but which conjured to my mind a macabre association of suicidally tempted elite.

Only by browsing through the *Discipline* could one turn up some of the following charming trivia: a detailed description of what it takes to qualify as a Methodist shrine and a list of the twelve buildings and sites that have been so designated, including "Wyandot Indian Mission, Upper Sandusky, Ohio," and "Acuff's Chapel, Highway 11-W between Blountville and Kingsport, Tennessee"; or that a Quarterly Conference might, if it considered such a Committee necessary to the work of a local church, establish a "Farm and Home Committee" for "assisting young couples to become established on the land and in small business inherent in the economy of the community, for the purpose of maintaining and strengthening the church community."

Other material in the *Discipline* remained as contemporary as the projected Farm and Home Committee was out of date: the suggestion that the Church should take its ministry to the beaches for the Easter migrations of college students; an endorsement of birth control, for the best kind of development in families and as a response to the world population explosion; an endorsement of compulsory seat belts in all new cars; and, in a section on Peace and World Order, commendation of United Nations programs and a plea for continued re-examination on the part of the United States of its attitude toward Mainland China.

Anyone who is interested in the Church's response to changing times can find, in the many editions of the Methodist *Discipline* since 1784 when the first *Discipline* was published, a telling reflection of the compromise and courage with which Methodists have tried to relate their faith and order to the life at hand.

We have, for good or ill, become much more enmeshed with the strands of the net that holds our worldly society together; whereas early Methodists could, as a radical fringe group, don their hair shirts and inveigh against the lack of fire and life in the established churches, we have now become one of those established churches, and we sometimes wonder whether the "controlled electric heating" of our newest church buildings describes more than the chill-removing unit in the basement. In the *Discipline* of 1784 the following paragraph appears:

Let all our churches be built plain and decent; but not more expensively than is absolutely unavoidable: Otherwise the necessity of raising money will make rich men necessary to us. But if so, we must be dependent on them, yea, and be governed by them. And then farewell to Methodist discipline, if not doctrine too.

But alas, by 1872, the *Discipline* capitulated to the pressures of worldly reality: the Civil War was over and a big Methodist building boom had begun, and Methodist discipline, if not doctrine too, would just have to take its chances amid the need for soliciting funds from any rich men we were fortunate enough to have in our burgeoning churches. The *Discipline* of 1872 retained its initial amorphous caution about plain and decent churches being built, with no more than necessary expense, but the cautions about being dependent on rich men were dropped and have never come back. So what has been called by some our "edifice complex" doth make cowards of us all.

A development, reflected in the *Discipline,* about which we can have less ambiguous feelings is the development in the rules pertaining to the marriage of divorced persons. When Hoyt first became a pastor, in 1954, the Methodist Church's ruling on divorce was unenlightened and unenforceable. The ruling read that a minister might not solemnize the marriage of a divorced person unless the person had been "the innocent party" in the defunct marriage and his or her innocence was "clearly established by competent testimony." Inasmuch as a broken marriage can scarcely ever be completely the fault of one person, leaving the other person "innocent," and inasmuch as the only testimony available to the minister approached by the divorced person seeking to be married usually comes from the partner who is trying to maintain his "innocence," his testimony can seldom be objectively convincing. At any rate, Hoyt and many of his colleagues classed this ruling with the prohibition against wearing gold and proceeded as Christian ministers to make their own judgments about persons coming to them requesting marriage.

By 1960 the Methodist Church had on this issue pulled ahead of civil law and the rules of most other churches, and at that time the *Discipline,* after stating the seriousness with which the Scriptures and the Church regard divorce, was changed to permit the minister to perform the marriage of divorced persons under this more realistic set of circumstances: when "(a) the divorced person is sufficiently aware of the factors leading to the failure of the previous marriage, (b) the divorced person is sincerely preparing to make the proposed marriage truly Christian, and (c) sufficient time has elapsed for adequate preparation and counseling."

I think it is hard to exaggerate the benefit which the considered blessing of the Church can bring to a person who still lives in the shadow of one broken marriage and waits hopefully—and perhaps somewhat fearfully—at the beginning of another, and one could wish the Methodist Church were as wise as this in all the rulings of the *Discipline.* You have only to listen over the telephone to the anxiety in the voice of a person who, making a first tentative inquiry and finding the minister not at home, may ask, "Well, do you know whether he ever marries people who have been divorced?" and then to hear the relief in the same voice when you have said, "Yes, he often does—can he call you about it when he gets home?" to know what a difference it makes to such persons to have the hope that the Church will stand with them in their new venture. And if it were possible to summon back to our time the ghost of John Wesley—to whom, in his time, the idea of divorce was surely anathema—can we not see him nod with approval as he reads Paragraph 356 of the *Discipline* of the Methodist Church, 1964, and finds here a new and compassionate witness to that old order from the General Rules, to "advise, reprove, comfort, or exhort, as occasion may require."

XII
The Doorbell Always Rings Twice

Everybody's doorbell rings. So does everybody's telephone. But ministers' doorbells and telephones ring oftener than other people's doorbells and telephones—at least it seems that way when the minister isn't home and his wife gets to do most of the answering. When he is there, since most of the telephone calls, at least, are for him, his wife is relieved of the need to answer so often and can get on with her work. Then the minister, who when he is at his office has a secretary to run interference for him, will say, "I wish the phone would stop ringing so I could get something done!" The minister's wife can smile brightly and say, "Yes, dear." The minister will get the message.

Now certainly I do not decry the invention of the telephone. As an instrument for health and safety, fellowship, and the saving of time, it is unbeatable. But, like every blessing, it has its complications, and the complications for ministers' wives have a pattern all their own.

There are people who call the minister's wife because they think the minister is too busy. "So I thought I'd explain it to you and you can tell him about it." This means double the work, as usually the wife knows nothing of the situation under discussion; she must write down all the details, lest she unknowingly leave out something important, and then try to recapitulate to the minister when he gets home. His attitude will be, "Get to the point. Get to the point"—but how do the uninitiated know which of the hundred details *is* the point?—and he will probably end up saying, "Why didn't he call me in the first place?" A good question, and I have acquired the habit of, where it is possible, stalling off the recital of the full details and suggesting to the caller that he or she call the office or leave a number for Hoyt to call later.

There are people who call me because they feel like chatting with someone and I have come to mind. I am reminded of the saying, "A person who has an hour to kill usually kills it with somebody who doesn't." Everyone of moderately sympathetic nature gets a certain number of these calls, and while they often do not coincide with the most convenient time for me to chat, I know what it is to wish for the diversion of a friendly voice, and I try to get into the spirit of the conversation. Besides, it is hard not to. One can say, "I'm mixing a cake. Can I call you back?" but it takes a lot more bravado to say, "I'm writing a book" or "I'm midway through a poem. Can I call you back?"

There are people who call because they want some minuscule bit of information on some church-related subject. They call the parsonage, say at 2:30 in the afternoon. When they find to their surprise that Hoyt is not here they ask me—some question like the location of an obscure Bible verse or some item on "what Methodists believe." I probably don't know the location of the Bible verse (though I can beat anyone in rapid recital of the names of the minor prophets, a skill I perfected at the age of eleven). I certainly am not qualified to launch into a discussion of the range of Methodist belief on almost any subject at all.

Or my caller may want information on some aspect of the church's program. Do I know whether the Parlor Furnishings Committee is meeting at 7:30 or at 8:00? Does "that meeting in Watertown" apply to all members of the Commission on Stewardship and Finance? I do know that Somebody is Doing Something about parlor furnishings and that there *is* a Commission on Stewardship and Finance, but that's as far as my knowledge goes.

Or someone will call and ask me whether Ronnie Eliot is home from the hospital yet. I don't know Ronnie Eliot, let alone that he is sick, let alone still more whether he is home from the hospital, to which he has evidently gone. If I confess my ignorance of these matters, I am met with the question, "Oh, didn't he tell you?" and I have to set about to maintain the image of my husband as someone who cares. (If he didn't tell you Ronnie Eliot is in the hospital, he must not care very much about poor Ronnie.) Of course he cares, and if Ronnie were very sick, or if I knew him at all well, my husband probably *would* have told me about it. But were he to fill me in on all the pastoral crises which come to his attention, we would have no time to talk together about things that do call for our attention, such as the welfare of our children, the state of our record player, and when we can go out to dinner. Furthermore, I would be involved in speculations about a lot of things that are just not my business. So usually I try to say, "Well, he probably mentioned it but I forgot," in which case I am the hardhearted one, but at least I am not the pastor, or, "He doesn't tell me about a lot of things that go on in the church," thus reinforcing the idea, which is true, that private matters confided to the minister stay with him alone, surely a more important value to preserve than for me to be informed on everything that goes on.

There are people who call out of some terrible need for help —an occasion of death or its prospect, a personal despair of finding meaning in life—and for these calls I will, of course, drop everything else in an effort to find where Hoyt is or to be of some help myself.

There are also people who call from full hearts to say what the minister's help and presence has meant to them or to someone they love, or to pass along a word of commendation from someone else, and these are occasions of glad affirmation for the minister and his wife, for a minister, too, is refreshed by the word of someone else that he is doing his work well.

There are occasional crank calls, people who, out of some distortion in their own nature, take it upon themselves to fill the minister in on a lot of gossipy details about some member of the church or to discourse at length on issues on which they think the minister needs enlightening. If I am home and he is not, it is to me that this unwanted harangue is delivered, and usually the best I can do is to let the speaker run down, interject an occasional cautionary comment, and, if he does not run down, to bring the conversation to a close with a promise that "I'll tell him."

While the telephone rings more often than the doorbell, the ringing of the doorbell can engage the minister's wife in situations more fully than can the most demanding message given over a telephone wire by an unseen voice.

The people who come to the parsonage door can be divided

into those who know that this is a church parsonage and those who do not. Representatives of either group can create situations of mild or serious crisis for the minister's wife who answers the door.

Among those who know are the members of the congregation. After the minister and his family have lived in the community for a while, the names of most of the members who come to church regularly will be known to them both. But not all the names of the members will be as familiar to the minister's wife as they are to the minister, nor will she know the names as quickly; she is probably not as skillful at associating names and faces and, of course, does not see the people anywhere nearly as often as her husband does. While the church members realize for the first month or so that this is the case, they may forget too soon. During that nebulous period of, say, about two months after the minister and his family have arrived in town until about a year after they have arrived, some church member is sure to show up at the parsonage door, bearing a gift. The minister's wife will sense that the gift bearer is, indeed, a member of the church. But she will not know his name. She will, of course, thank him effusively for the gift. But how to tell her husband who the donor is so that he, too, may thank the person for the gift? A description of a "fifty-ish-looking man, medium height, receding hairline, a little heavy," probably describes half the members of the Official Board, let alone the other men in the church, any one of whom may be the donor. Furthermore, the man's wife, if he has a wife, should be thanked. Has he a wife? The situation is immeasurably worse if the gift is wrapped, as certainly the contents must be acknowledged with a note to the family, and to whom to send the note? The best recourse to this dilemma, after all hunches have been exhausted, is to hope to see the gentleman again soon, in the company of a lady who one hopes is his wife, to thank these persons again for the gift, and, if the minister is present, to communicate to him by mutually understood signs such as "We've surely enjoyed *those lovely pears* you gave us" that this is the mystery couple, so he can add his thanks on the spot and then tell you later who the people are.

Another kind of crisis arises when a member of the congregation rings the doorbell and the minister's wife must go to the door in some condition which is par for the course for every other woman in the community but which is somehow not what one would expect to find in a minister's wife. I measure the recovery powers of a gentleman at the door by the way in which he responds to the spectacle of the minister's wife with rollers in her hair. If I sense that the person on the other side of the door is embarrassed I say, with what I hope is a disarming smile, "Excuse the curlers." This shows that I, too, know that I am wearing curlers, and that I, too, know it is a little awkward of me to appear this way. One poor man responded to my effort to put him at ease by not only continuing to look the other way, but by carrying on the subject he had started on, with no acknowledgment that I had spoken of the hair rollers at all.

On one occasion I was midway through the process of combing and setting my just-washed hair when the doorbell rang. I answered it and there stood a young man, a member of the church and fortunately a good friend. He observed the situation —I, with a damp towel slung around the shoulders of a blooming maternity smock, my wet hair combed straight except for squiggles of remaining permanent at the ends—and, after a quizzical moment, said, "Hello, you gorgeous creature," which remains my favorite opener for a minister's-wife-at-the-door scene.

One slight camouflage to the hair rollers would be one of those bouffant elasticized caps made for the purpose, but if you have a round face anyway, a bouffant bonnet sliding halfway down it is not an improvement and just compounds the comedy. Of course I could try to curl my hair at night. But I couldn't sleep with today's hair-styling apparatus on my head, and besides my husband has enough problems during the daytime without having to sleep with someone who looks like an unidentified lying object.

Sometimes the doorbell rings and I am confronted, as on the telephone, by someone who expects me to have more information than I have. "Will you please sign for these twenty packages and where shall I put them?" Or, "Someone called about the mimeograph. When can I get in the office to fix it?" I once answered the door to find a Salvation Army truck driver, who had come for "those chairs you called about." I didn't know what chairs he meant. I had heard some talk about "chairs from the choir room" being about to be given away. Inasmuch as the driver and truck had made a special trip out from town to pick up the chairs, I felt I should try not to send him back empty-handed. He must mean the chairs in the choir loft, which were in bad shape. I couldn't leave my babies to go with him, but he seemed like a reliable fellow, so I told him where the chairs were and gave him the church key. When he returned the key he assured me that yes, he had taken the chairs I described.

When Hoyt came home I reported to him how I had used my good judgment in this crisis. He charged out of the house to check on which chairs were gone. The man had indeed taken the chairs I described, but they were the wrong chairs to have given away. The chairs the church planned to replace were some still more decrepit chairs which were stacked in a little alcove behind the choir loft; this was "the choir room." So, Hoyt must call to ask the Salvation Army to return our chairs in trade for the correct ones. The next day the same driver appeared again. I gave him the key with apologies for the mistake, and he went and switched the chairs and returned the key to me. About a week later the church decided that these chairs, too, were in sad condition and should be given away after all. This time Hoyt stayed home to greet the driver and negotiate about the key. I couldn't go through it again.

Some people who come to the church parsonage knowing that it is a church parsonage are transients looking for money, work, or food, and they have learned by some inquiry or transient underground that a minister lives here.

What to do? If there is a center for transients in town, one can always send such a person there. Often there is no such place, and maybe a glimpse of home could be an agent for rehabilitating a drifter in society. We know that a handout of some kind may only reinforce patterns of drifting, but what is a Christian to do when a person in need comes to his door? We know there are men who become rich living as derelicts and playing on the sympathies and guilt feelings of more responsible citizens. How is a person to know who is "sincere" and who is not, and of what does "sincerity" consist under conditions of a life without roots or true security of any kind? We know that a minister—or his wife—cannot reorganize his whole life around the rehabilitation of a dropout from society who comes to his door—and a major reorganization of one's life is about what it would take—and even then chances of making a significant change in such a person's life pattern are slim. I think that most ministers and their wives have wrestled with this problem in its various forms and are perhaps never really happy with whatever compromise solution they choose. What *is* the Christian response to the appeal of a drifter at the door? A man whose opinion we highly respect on questions of human relationships said to me once, "I *never* give money. I *always* give food."

So, what to do? We have turned people away and later wished we had not. We have helped people by whom we later discovered we had been taken in—people who played a confidence game on the sympathy and sense of obligation of ministers. And there have been transients whom we have received into the family—particularly if there are children involved. I recall a man who with his wife and baby stopped at our parsonage one afternoon in need of food and money to continue on their way. (They always have an offer of a job if they can just get to the next town, and an amazing number, at least while they are at our house, are Methodists.) So we fed them, and Hoyt bought them bus tickets for the next lap of their journey, and I gave the mother a dress to replace the soiled and worn one she was wearing. But what really brought this family out of the stereotype of "the transient family" was the baby. The baby was crying and the mother said, while she was changing its diaper, that the child had a bad case of diaper rash and she couldn't seem to clear it up. I gave her a tube of ointment of the kind I found most soothing for my baby, and she put some on the child and the baby stopped crying. The woman and I sat and talked together in mutual gratitude about our children. Is there a mother in the world whose heart is not made lighter when a baby stops crying and is happy again?

I recall another man who with his wife and three children shared a hastily extended supper with us one evening. My young cousin, a child brought up in relative affluence, was visiting us, and I noticed that she didn't eat much. She had a healthy appetite, and after the family had left I asked her if she wasn't hungry. She said, "Yes, but when I saw how they went for the food I thought I could wait until another time." After supper Hoyt drove the family to the nearby town where "a friend" had rented a room for them in a cheap hotel; the friend was to show up with work for the man the next day. The next afternoon, in the midst of a heavy snowstorm, the man appeared at the door again. He had walked the five miles out from town in the snowstorm. He was apologetic to be bothering us again, but the friend wasn't going to get there until tomorrow, and his family hadn't eaten anything all day, and he wondered if we could help him again.

We gave him as much food as he could carry; he refused the offer of a ride back to town, and when we queried him about the walk and the cold and the weight of the bag he said, "Food for his family never weighs very heavy in a man's arms." Hoyt gave him a little money, which the man insisted he would send back when he could. He did not send it back, and we didn't expect him to. I suppose that family went on in this pattern of life, and the number of such families is legion. Of course our bit of help to them was only a stopgap, and of course such actions can easily become a salve for our consciences when we should be working at the remaking of society, though I think involvement with such people makes us more rather than less eager for reform in society. But is one to deny a cup of cold water because he is aggravating a statistic?

So much for those who come to the parsonage knowing it is a parsonage. A lot of different situations arise with those who come not knowing. In many cases, the fact that this is a parsonage makes no difference at all—calls for the United Fund and other charitable organizations, girls selling Girl Scout cookies, people making surveys or campaigning for election. In some cases I much prefer the caller not know this is a parsonage. If someone comes selling chances, our refusal to buy them is perhaps slightly more disconcerting if it is not known that a minister lives here, as ministers are "supposed to be against gambling." And if the Avon lady comes and I want to buy false eyelashes or blue eye shadow I can do so without dislodging her image of the entire Christian enterprise.

Sometimes the fact that this is a parsonage can be brought out as an ace up one's sleeve. This is particularly true if someone comes around trying to sell a new roof, siding for the house, or other home improvement. The minister's wife has only to say, "This is a church parsonage," and the sales pressure is gone; everyone knows churches do not make unpremeditated decisions about major repairs on parsonages. Besides, salesmen are often intimidated by a minister's wife, as though arguing with her is like arguing with absolute truth—an impression I try not to destroy.

There are some salesmen, however, for whom the image of the minister's wife as a person with whom one does not argue cuts no ice. Chief among such brave persons are ardent members of other sectarian groups, such as Jehovah's Witnesses.

Now, I have the greatest respect for anyone who will conquer his reticence and fear of rejection enough to go out and proclaim his religion to the unconverted. And in a way these people are members of the brotherhood, and would—or so I thought—have some spark of special comradeship toward ministers and their wives. So it came as something of a surprise to me to discover that, in the eyes of Jehovah's Witnesses, I am just another heathen. The "this is a parsonage; I am a minister's wife" gambit got no light in the eye from them. I got the same Scripture verses, the same threats of doom, the same non sequiturs, the same bulldozer one-way conversation as anyone else. So, I am polite. I try to be responsive not to the message but to the person. I have even engaged in long conversations with representatives of Jehovah's Witnesses when I felt they approached me as a person rather than a target. I regret very much that there seems so little possibility of a meeting of spirits in persons who are so committed to their religion. But I am not interested in being the focus of a one-way blast.

On at least one occasion Hoyt was home when the representative of Jehovah's Witnesses rang the doorbell, and, feeling in a companionable and sparring mood, he invited the Witness to come in and discourse with him. The visitor stayed an hour and a half. From time to time I came to the hall to eavesdrop and to enjoy Hoyt's ability to introduce some order into this verbal joust. But it's not for me. When I am accosted at the front door by a tract-bearing Witness with a predetermined eye and a canned speech, I listen graciously to the first—perhaps the second—stage of the speech and then I say, "I am a Methodist, and I believe in my religion just as much as you believe in yours. I appreciate your willingness to come, but I am not interested." It seems to me sometimes that with this honesty the guard drops just a little. And I think what a shell these people have to build around themselves to persist in making these calls when they are in many places made to feel so unwelcome.

Apart from the religious salesmen who come not knowing—and who are unintimidated to learn—that this is a parsonage, I think the most extroverted individual I have ever met was also a salesman who came to the door and whose bravura sustained only a momentary quiver when I produced what I thought would be a final discouragement—that I was a minister's wife.

To begin with this gentleman arrived at 5:45 in the afternoon, a most inauspicious time to be maknig sales calls on anyone. I had stayed too long at my sewing and was hurrying along with dinner preparations. The children had been cutting out magazine pictures in the living room, and the floor was littered with papers. The doorbell rang, and I went to answer it. There stood two young men: one burly, smiling, and open-faced; the other smaller, more diffident, looking hesitant about being here.

"Hello," I said.

"Hello," said the open-faced young man. "Did you happen to watch *See the People* on TV last night?"

"No," I said, happy to disqualify myself from whatever was brewing. He looked startled, almost hurt. "I don't watch much television," I said, apologizing. I looked at the folder under his arm. "But if you're selling anything, we're not interested."

"Oh." He was bright again. "I'm not *selling* subscriptions," he said, and then, "I'm Jeff Stoner." I nodded. "What's your name?" he asked.

"Mrs. Hickman."

Jeff nodded. "Oh," he said, "and this is my friend, Louie." Louie was looking glumly at the floor. "Smile, Louie," Jeff said, giving Louie a jab in the ribs with his elbow and smiling double wattage himself.

Louie said, "Ugh," faintly, and smiled. I nodded again, at

Louie. He looked as though he needed encouragement, just to stay alive.

Jeff started in again. "Do you get the *Ladies' Home Journal?*" he said.

"Yes, I do," I said brightly.

"Oh." I could tell he was disappointed again. But he gathered himself together and said, suddenly, "Oh, are you at least twenty-one years old?"

I was thirty-five at the time and at 5:45 in the afternoon I looked it. "Yes," I said, smiling in spite of myself. I looked at Louie, who was maintaining his calm. "Smile, Louie," I said.

Jeff and Louie looked at each other. Jeff gave a young man's version of a giggle, took a deep breath, audibly, and started in again. "Well, you'd go along with your neighbors here, wouldn't you? Do you know Mr. Farley?"

"No," I said, which was true—we hadn't lived here long.

Jeff was not daunted. "Well, you'd go along with your neighbors here in giving me twenty-five cents a week for delivering three of these magazines—" He pulled a crumpled list from his pocket. He saw I was about to protest. "I'm not selling subscriptions," he said. "The magazines are free. The quarter is just for delivery."

"Oh," I said. "Well, we have all the magazines we need."

"How about children's magazines?" Jeff said. "Do you have children?"

Louie shifted his foot. He was looking at the room beyond us, its floor littered with scraps of paper, scissors, and four now attentive children. "No," he said in a hollow voice. "No, she don't have any children."

But Jeff had heard something else—the noise of someone typing upstairs. "Who's that typing upstairs?" he said.

"That's my husband," I said.

"Is he a manager or something?"

"No," I said.

He repeated the question. "Is he a manager?"

"No," I said, "he's a minister."

Jeff was awed. For a good thirty seconds he was really subdued. He looked at me, his eyes wide. "Honest?" he said.

I thought, Aha, my ace has worked again. But I underestimated Jeff. A new light came into his eyes. He moved a step forward toward the bottom of the stairs. He turned to me. "Whaddya call him—Reverend Hickman?"

It was my turn to smile. "No, I don't call him Reverend Hickman," I said.

Jeff looked at Louie. Then at me. "I mean what should *I* call him—Reverend Hickman?"

"If you like," I said.

Jeff put his foot on the bottom step. "Reverend *Hick*man," he shouted. After one such bellow, the typing stopped and Hoyt came down. Jeff started in about the magazines: he wasn't selling subscriptions, the twenty-five cents a week was just a delivery fee. "Your wife thought she didn't need any more. But I thought maybe you. . . ."

By now the children were immobilized on the floor by the spectacle. I went into the dining room to finish setting the table. I should have gone to the kitchen, but I was afraid I would miss something.

Finally I heard Hoyt pull out *his* magazine salesman ace.

"Well, you see," he said, "I have access to a magazine agency, too; I can get magazines at a reduced rate myself."

"Well," Jeff said, "maybe you'd like to pay me a quarter just to have me drop in—just for my personality." But the jig was up and he knew it. "Nice to have met you," he said, and we all smiled and grunted at each other. Even, as the door closed behind him, Louie smiled.

Of course Jeff was the first man out.

XIII
How to Avoid Having
to Have a Dog

It all started because we didn't want to have a dog. Ministers move around too much, and in the city a dog has to be fenced in or kept on a leash or in the house. Besides, I like to know where things are, and a dog wanders around the house so, and I might be musing at my typewriter and find the dog under my desk. Besides that, having gone through the necessary details with four children, I don't want to have to start house-training a dog. I know I'd be the only one with sufficient motivation to keep at it, and I'm just temperamentally unsuited to swatting dogs with rolled-up newspapers, which is what I understand you have to do to train dogs effectively. And what would we do with a dog on our long and lovely vacations? I am not that fond of animals to want to share the interior of a car with five other people and a possibly carsick dog. And boarding kennels are expensive, especially when one's husband is a minister and has therefore a month's vacation.

But we knew the children should have some kind of pet. Having a pet encourages children to be responsible and all that. And they love pets, and we want them to be happy and not to grow up remembering a childhood filled with resentment and deprivation because they weren't allowed to have a pet. (I at least have enough anxiety about being an adequate parent that I'm fair game for any threat to an anxious parent's anxiety.) Besides, there was the moving. A pet would help the children feel at ease with the moving, and everybody knows Methodist ministers move.

We didn't start out with pets right away. A couple of times we moved with a baby due imminently, and that was diversion enough. And in those early years the children were so little they didn't know what they were missing. But with the first move after we stopped having babies, the pet conversations and requests became more and more urgent.

But no dog. Please, no dog. Let's have something that doesn't wander around, something we can keep in a box or a cage.

Of course Hoyt thought of turtles. Hadn't he kept at one time or another about fifty turtles, for fifteen years, through winter hibernations (the turtles') and summer trips (his)? He went to the local pet store and, connoisseur of what gives a turtle health and adaptability, he picked what must have been the two hardiest turtles in the tank. For these two turtles survived and grew, through many a change in locale and shifts in hours of sunshine, through many discards of blackened wooden rafts, through many boxes of turtle food, offerings of dead flies, and occasional leftover vegetables.

The turtles, animate and entertaining, were sufficient pets for quite a while. If we yearned for companionship with dogs there were always the neighbors' dogs, to be enjoyed from a friendly and irresponsible distance. (It did startle us one day to have Mary come home and report that she had heard the family across the street call to its new dog—highly pedigreed and recently imported from England—and she thought they had named the dog "Reverend." We were quite certain these neighbors bore us no animosity, but just the same I was reassured when later that day I heard the dog summoned again and heard the young wife call out loud and clear, "Reverie! Here, Reverie.")

Our next move after the acquisition of the turtles was not only to a new city but to a temporary house. We were to live in the church's present parsonage only a few months, until a new parsonage could be located and readied for occupancy. In this state of suspended housing and semiunpacked boxes, sufficient extra anxiety seems to have been generated to have called for extra action in the pet department.

The first new pet was a chameleon. For what reason I do not remember, the chameleon became Stephen's. Maybe he put some of his earnings toward its purchase. Maybe it was given to him on the theory that the two older boys owned the two turtles, or because he seemed to have the most new-school anxiety to allevi-ate. Maybe it was just by birthright, because Stephen has an empathy for and an interest in small creatures that is hard to exaggerate. He has been an ant-watcher since he could first crawl to the edge of his outdoor playpen and look over the side. If there is a creek anywhere within walking distance of any place he lands in, he will find it, as lemmings find the sea. If there is a small swimming creature—just one—in the creek, he will find that. He has found crayfish in creeks where long-term residents of the area have assured him there were no visible creatures of any kind. He has found tiny frogs on tops of mountains. We do

not start out on rides in the country, or to picnic grounds of unknown configuration, that he does not have his equipment with
him. (His motto: "Security is having your net and your jar.")
And almost invariably we return from outings with Stephen,
feet wet and muddy, happily clutching his jar full of sloshing
water and tiny creatures.

I think the chameleon was the first any of us had ever seen,
and we were fascinated. Yes, it did change its color to conform
to the background—though, honestly, a higher form of life like
a person would never have difficulty distinguishing a chameleon
from a tree branch. You couldn't say the chameleon was *affec-
tionate,* exactly, but it did react to its environment to the extent
of this skin-altering tour de force, and it didn't have that anti-
social turtle habit of pulling in its head and closing down the
house if you wanted to talk and it didn't. Stephen named the
chameleon Henry, and it lived in the parsonage dining room in
a high-sided glass dish.

Of course Henry had to eat. The pet store, and the booklet,
"Enjoy Your Chameleon," which Hoyt had bought along with
Henry, suggested a diet of live mealworms. Mealworms are a
form of life known to laymen as grubworms. If allowed to, they
spawn in garbage cans in the summer. They become flies. They
are enough to send a shudder through any even mildly fastidious
housewife. This was the recommended diet for chameleons. Hoyt
brought home a box: mealworms packed in fine sawdust. Furthermore—he told me this with some misgiving—they should be
kept in the refrigerator. Where else? Otherwise the mealworms
would not survive. At fifty cents a box, some scruples would
have to go. I assigned a section of a seldom-used door shelf to

the mealworm box, so I wouldn't always be moving the mealworms to get at the butter.

But alas, before we had gone through many boxes, and while we were still in the temporary house, the chameleon died, the ecology of the dining room, even with a diet of mealworms, evidently not being right to support a chameleon who had always looked rather frail.

The children, with Hoyt's help, buried the chameleon and then went back to the pet store. They returned bearing a small gray scaly creature, about three inches long, with flat, pointed protrusions extending back from its head, and with stark and blinking eyes. This, they told me enthusiastically, was a horned toad, to replace poor Stephen's poor dead chameleon. They had also purchased the relevant booket, "Enjoy Your Horned Toad." When we asked Stephen what he was going to name the horned toad, he said, "His name is Henry."

In a variation of the bread and butter game—since the deceased chameleon had left us with half a box of mealworms extant—the horned toad also ate mealworms, or live flies in season. It soon became evident that, while Henry certainly would eat mealworms, he preferred live flies. Not only that, but his performance in eating live flies was so much more entertaining than that involved in the simple observing and gulping down of a cold (and therefore lethargic) mealworm, that flies became for the observers, too, the preferred menu. Henry would spot the fly, would freeze to immobility except for his darting eyes, and, when the fly had alit, with a lunge and a lightning-quick extension of his incredibly flexible tongue would reach, gulp, and swallow. The process of catching the fly in a net, transferring it to Henry's dish, slipping a lid over the dish to prevent the fly's escape, and then watching Henry eat this delicacy made the feeding of Henry his several flies a day a major summer activity.

One evening we returned from a ride to find Henry missing from his dish. We searched in all the closets and corners and under all the furniture. We even took up floor registers and looked underneath into the metal ducts to see if we could find him. But no Henry. When we had exhausted all places to look and ourselves as well, we all went to bed, half listening still for some mysterious rustle, and hoping Henry would show up.

The next morning I was sitting in the bay window reading the morning paper and enjoying a post-breakfast cup of coffee when I heard a fast "swoosh" and then a thud right beside my chair. I looked up and there on the floor beside the chair was Henry, temporarily inert but unharmed. He must have climbed up the window drapery and spent the night on top of the window, from which perch, whether from fatigue or choice, he had just now relinquished his hold and slid back down to rejoin the family.

As soon as the rejoicing subsided, Hoyt took the children back to the pet store to purchase an escape-proof home for Henry: a glass vivarium (a dry aquarium) with, in accordance with a suggestion from "Enjoy Your Horned Toad," a reflector light, which during the cold fall and winter months ahead would more nearly simulate the Arizona desert that was Henry's natural habitat.

In this warm, sandy, fly-visited milieu, Henry lived, absorbing such water as he needed by lying in the small pan of it we kept in his cage. He became a traveled horned toad; though he never returned to the Arizona desert, he went with us on the full extent of our summer vacation one year, his tank slid into the cargo space of the station wagon, where he seemed a pleasant diversion for whichever child was having his turn riding back there. Then, in the middle of one winter, Henry began to appear more and more sluggish, and one day he was observed to have died.

Our next step was to add a hamster. We bought one male hamster at the same pet store which had yielded up the chameleon and the horned toad. And of course we bought a hamster cage, with exercise wheel, water bottle, and resting shelf. And a bag of cedar shavings and, this time, boxes of prepared hamster food, and yet another booklet: "Enjoy Your Hamster."

The hamster had more personality than the chameleon, though not more than Henry the Inscrutable, and seemed more approachable than the turtles. Hoyt and I had fond associations with hamsters. One of our friends in the church group where we had met each other had kept pet hamsters, and he used to bring them to youth meetings and break everyone up by fishing them out of his suit pockets at opportune times, like while we were having doughnuts and coffee after Sunday evening meetings.

After ensconcing the first hamster in his cage, and upon perusing carefully the booklet, "Enjoy Your Hamster," we realized that hamsters like company; they are sociable little fellows and enjoy having one of their own kind around. Since our first hamster had been sold to us as a male, we decided to have the second a male also, as we didn't want to start raising baby hamsters. Our two bachelors, after a few moments of mutual hesitation, seemed to get along well and frolicked in their cage with great sociability. But one morning we found that our new hamster, #2 hamster, had escaped from the cage during the night. We never found him. This was the house that was due for demolition, and an adroit cow could have got out one of the holes in the basement, let alone a tiny creature like a hamster. After a reasonable period of mourning we got a third hamster, again specifying male, so what was our surprise, a few weeks later, upon giving a casual glance toward the hamsters one evening, to find a batch of tiny semitransparent babies lying about in the cage.

Now, it is very hard to tell the lady hamsters from the gentlemen. I have a friend with a Master's Degree in zoology, and *she* says it is hard to tell the ladies from the gentlemen. But you'd think the pet store could have told the difference.

We were now faced with a crisis. The hamster book said that if a mother hamster has babies you must immediately remove the father from the cage or he will destroy the babies. On the theory that the third hamster must have introduced the divergence of sex—otherwise (if either #1 or #2 had been female) we'd have had babies before—we left hamster #3 with the babies and removed hamster #1 from the cage. Hamsters, being mammals, nurse their young, and we waited for the nourishment to begin. We also got a second hamster cage (with water bottle, exercise wheel, and resting shelf) to house the banished father.

The mother seemed to ignore the babies. After a day passed we tried putting drops of warm milk to the babies' mouths, but they didn't respond. Eventually the babies died. In a truly agonizing post-mortem of this sorry affair we learned that we had removed the wrong hamster from the cage. Our friend the zoologist confirmed it. As a mother myself, I am filled with anguish even yet by the memory of this disaster.

After the babies died we reunited the parents. It may have been my imagination, but it seemed to me that the mother suffered some kind of psychic damage through all this: she remained highly nervous (hamsters are nervous creatures anyway) and unamenable to socializing, either with us or with the other hamster, and the first time one of the boys left the door of the cage sufficiently insecured that she could work it up and get out, she did so, and we never found her again, either, though by now we were living in our "new" parsonage, the walls and the basement were tight, there were no known cracks in the backs of closets, and we didn't know where she could have gone.

In the meantime, being somewhat heartsick on the whole subject of hamsters and wanting to supplement the pet population with something less reminiscent of failure, we had got Stephen a white guinea pig for his birthday—plus cage, plus hay, plus feeding bowls, plus various other dietary items, plus another volume in the series, this one entitled, "Enjoy Your Guinea Pig." Now, guinea pigs are a definite upgrading in terms of responsiveness from turtles, chameleons, hamsters, and horned toads, and Stephen's delight at this small white guinea pig and all its antics was genuine, constant, and catching—so catching that, as soon as occasion allowed, Mary and Peter (John owned the surviving hamster) acquired guinea pigs, too: a male for Peter, a female for Mary.

We now had the turtles, the hamster, and three guinea pigs. And, oh, yes, the goldfish won in a giveaway drawing at school. The teacher had found goldfish a nuisance to take care of, and after some of them died in rapid succession she had put the lone survivor up for grabs—and Mary had drawn the lucky number. But we still had no dog or cat. Nothing that you couldn't keep in a box or cage. Nothing that would tear around messing up the Methodist parsonage or, more to the point, be a constant

care for the minister's wife. Nothing that required a leash, or a
fenced-in yard. Nothing that some indulgent friend or neighbor
wouldn't board for vacation, if you didn't want to take it with
you. When we went away on vacation, Hoyt took the turtles and
the hamster to his church office, where the long-suffering custodian would shake in daily allotments of food and murmur a
few communal words. On one of our vacations this same friend
agreed to keep the guinea pigs at his home for us, and when we
came back he had evolved a personality profile and a pet name
for each one.

By now the acquisition of guinea pigs—and the question of
pets in general—had lost all relationship to the threats and con-
solations involved in moving. Certainly the issue of moving
meant nothing to the guinea pigs! To them the calls of nature
and no issues of more subtle psychological need were the deter-
minants of life. In due time we had our first batch of guinea pigs,
and no parents of human infants were, I think, more excited or
pleased than our children were over these new baby pets.

We realized, of course, that we couldn't keep indefinite numbers of indefinitely multiplying guinea pigs. As soon as the babies
were old enough to leave their mother ("Enjoy Your Guinea
Pigs" suggested four weeks), we found homes for the baby
guinea pigs among the children's friends, maintained a propri-
etary interest in these babies in their new homes, and enjoyed an
image of ourselves as bestowers of joy and cultivators of responsibility among the children to whose homes our guinea pigs had
gone.

But in due course of time we acquired another, and another,
and another litter of guinea pigs, and we began to use up our
available friends as prospective homes for guinea pigs. Even

friends of friends who could be prevailed on to take a guinea pig became harder to find. Many came to exclaim, and hope, but parents were not always as enthusiastic. We began offering our guinea pigs to the pet shop, to the local zoo, and even to the County Humane Society, should someone come to them looking for a pet guinea pig. We also began separating the boys from the girls, both in the indoor boxes and cages in which the guinea pigs lived most of the time and in the outdoor pens we had constructed of wooden pegs and rounds of fencing, so in good weather the guinea pigs could munch fresh grass and enjoy the sunshine. By now we had lost track of the generations, as well as all potential for being scandalized at the amorous proclivities for one another of mothers and sons, of fathers and cousins and daughters.

The guinea pigs brought their share of sorrow to the family, too. One winter, before we had learned from the veterinarian that we should provide them with extra vitamins in winter, several of the guinea pigs died. Another time a mother and one of her babies died two days after the babies' birth. The weather had turned suddenly cold overnight, the mother appeared to be failing, and an emergency trip to the pet hospital and an injection of antibiotic did not revive her. And one day the patriarch of the guinea pig family, Stephen's original Nibbles, who had been the object of Stephen's devotion for the three and a half years of the guinea pig's life with us and who had been observed to have some signs of old age, was found dead in his box, and a grief fell over the household of an immediacy and desolation I had forgotten since the long years of my childhood when my brother's pet dog had been killed on an icy road one winter night and there had been no consolation for us, either.

With deaths in the guinea pig family, and gifts of baby guinea pigs to all who were willing to receive them, our guinea pig population is down now to a second-generation father, housed in his box in the garage, and the infant whom we've been feeding with a medicine dropper since his mother died the second day after his birth. When he was tiny the boys took him upstairs with them at night, so when he squeaked from hunger they could wake and feed him—a good preparation for their fatherhood. But now he can eat pellets and does not need his droppers full of milk every hour or so. In fact he is now so fat we watch him daily lest he outgrow the hamster cage but be too big to get out the cage door, and we have to call the fire department.

We still have the turtles and the goldfish. We have Stephen's current collection of protozoa and tiny fish, and a new Henry, a growing garter snake, found one afternoon at a picnic gathering of clergy families. This Henry has already rewarded Stephen's interest in biology and natural phenomena by shedding his skin, which, in its parchment-thin, snake-shaped form, now adorns the screen covering the top of the aquarium where Henry lives. This Henry has escaped a couple of times, too—once onto the bureau top, and once into the back recesses of the boys' closet, from which he gave his location away by rustling around in a piece of tissue paper, causing Stephen to say fondly, "Poor Henry. He must have been tired."

We have a new booklet now, "Enjoy Your Cat." No, we didn't move again. No one seemed in particular need of anxiety-alleviating pets. But Mary has wanted a kitty for a long time. It is a good idea for her, being the youngest, to have something small and cuddly to take care of. And a kitty can live happily inside, and can train itself, and is less trouble to take care of than a dog. So now we have this black cat, named Velvet. He is playful and long-suffering, and the children love him. Every morning he mews outside the door at the top of the stairs. He comes rubbing around our legs, and then does his "lie down and die act" —an apparent effort to appear weak and helpless—when he is hungry. He ignores his bed and sleeps on the afghan or, in the daytime, on one of the children's beds.

I suppose it had to come sometime, this graduation to more mobile animals, though it does seem that life was simpler before. Now I'm wondering: the next time we move, what will happen then? Will it be a chihuahua or a German shepherd?

XIV
We'll Be Home Tomorrow

Well, we are moving again. I am not really surprised. We talked about it last spring and thought we'd stay here one more year.

All year as I have done the seasonal things, as the months have come and gone, I have thought about it; with fall and school reopening, and the Hallowe'en costumes taken out of the box in the attic and improvised for another year, I have thought about it.

As the first snow has come and the last bird flock has perched like dark leaves on the branches of the elm tree and then with a chirp, in a whirr, in an instant, has sprung loose from the tree and swirled in a black feathering to the south, I have thought about it.

As we have had our flu shots and taken down our Christmas tree and shopped for coats in the January sales, as the big snows have melted and then a Sunday afternoon in March has come when we have taken our kites down to the field at the end of our street, I have thought about it.

As we have pushed up our storm panels and blown out the musty air of winter and made yet another try at keeping the spring mud from tracking into the house, I have thought about it.

As the spring lunch for school mothers has come around and the strange mystery of Eastertime has plunged the church into its Lenten activity, as the last week of school has come with its home-bringing of desk loads of art work and its notebooks of penmanship and the year's final report cards, this time not to be returned; with all these signs of the passing of the year I have thought, It may be the last time for this house, it may be the last time for here.

And now we *are* going to move, and I should have been prepared. I am not surprised, but I am never prepared. Twice, as a church has bought a new parsonage, we have moved from one house to another in the same town, and these moves were not hard. But the others, the pulling up of the family—the two of us, then the three, the four, and the five, the six of us—have all been terrible. I am willing to go, and I look forward to the new city and the new adventures and alignments. The starting all over is an opportunity many people do not have, and I'm glad to put down community responsibilities here and decide again what I want to do in a new place. I know that moving frequently is part of American life, and that many families do not move into the built-in welcome waiting for a minister's family. But just the same it is terrible.

I joke about it. I tell my friends they can expect me to cry. I say, "If I could just take a two-months' sleeping pill it would be all right." I know that I will like the new community when I get settled there; we have never moved to a community where this has not been true. But it has always seemed to me some violation of natural security for a family to put all the objects of its life together into a lot of cardboard boxes and see them loaded onto a truck and driven off with, to be received and re-instated in some alien dwelling. I know that the strength of a family does not depend upon where its books are put in relation to its sofa, or whether you reach for the frying pan to the left of the stove or to the right of it. But let us not minimize, either, the grooves these patterns make in whatever matrix shapes our security.

Hoyt does not mind as much as I do. I am not surprised, and I am glad that he doesn't. I suppose it is always harder for a woman to move; her roots go down into the particular earth she walks upon, morning after morning, afternoon after afternoon, evening after evening. Over this walk I have carried my clothes basket. My children are related by the ecstasies and curiosities of childhood to the blades of grass in this back yard, to the way these stones are piled on one another at the base of this apple tree. How can we give it all away and start again?

It was to this room I brought my daughter home from the hospital. In this driveway my son taught himself to ride a bicycle, up and down and around, falling off and getting on again. Here we planted our garden of lettuce and mint and watched it with the pride of a farmer surveying his hundred acres. To this west window we have all come on the summons of whichever child saw it first and called to us, "Come and see the sunset!" How can we give it all away?

I know where the groceries are in the store I go to. I know the doctor's telephone number. I know which hills to avoid if I have to drive in slippery weather. I know where the safe places are for the children to play, and who their friends are. I know all the teachers in the school. I know where we can find blackberries in the summer and rhubarb in the spring. And now we are going to move.

I call the mover. Over the phone and later when he comes to look at our things I am very efficient. "About eight rooms," I say, "and quite a lot in the attic. Yes, a piano. A refrigerator but no freezer. And my husband estimates about a thousand books." He leaves me the cartons, stacked flat, in the corner.

Hoyt usually does the books. I do most of the rest, except for the best dishes, and the movers will come a day early and do those for us. Many things, happily, can go as they are. We will fill all the empty spaces in drawers, we will put sofa pillows on the shelves of the china closet when the goblets have been packed. I put a big box in the corner of each bedroom, and we put the toys and other loose things in the bottom and leave space for the last-minute bedding on top. I pack the least-used kitchen things early—the scale, the cookie press, the steamer, the turkey roaster. A lot of things have to wait until the last week. My neighbor comes and helps me, for I am bogged down in my compulsion for organizing it all efficiently. "You'll find it when you get there," she says, and puts things into the box and marks it with a big K. I'm not usually this compulsive, I know. It's just my way of trying to put it off.

I have had three strep throats in a row, and I think these, too, are my way of trying to put it off; my throat feels so constricted I don't see how blood can flow freely there at all, though I suppose it does.

I am sick with a fever on our last Sunday with the church—though we will not move for another ten days—so I cannot go to the services. I am torn between my regret at not being with my family and my relief at not having to sit through the sacred familiar services in this sacred familiar room and know it is for the last time. But I have a fever and the question answers itself. Hoyt records the service for me and brings back the tape, and in the afternoon I play it back. At one point I detect a break in Hoyt's voice, as he tells the congregation we will be moving. Dear love, I think. It is not easy for you. For all your enthusiasm about the move it is not easy for you. And I wonder that he is so strong, that his voice breaks, slightly, only once. But I am a coward; this is not my kind of bravery, and I am grateful for my fever and that I did not have to go.

With this move, the children are old enough to help with some of their things. They pack their games and books and some of the contents of the playroom. They are excited about the move —the prospect of a new house and the adventure of a new city, and on a Great Lake, too! We talk about all the swimming and fishing we will do, and we learn that you can hire canoes and go through the lagoons on the edge of the bay. We look on our state map to see the locations of the nearby national parks, and we plan which we shall go to first. They know that part of my enthusiasm is forced, that I am whistling to keep up my courage, but they are accustomed to Mother's rises and falls and accept this, kindly, as what is to be expected of me. They know there may be some hard times for them, too. The shyest of the children and the most talkative seem to have more misgivings than the other two: the shy one because friends are slowly acquired and dear; the gregarious one because friends are omnipresent and important. I talk to each of them separately, reassuring him that he will make friends again.

We have our farewell dinner and all the nice things are said, and I do not cry until nearly the end. One of the boys sustains me—I have told the children I shall probably cry and they are not to be surprised, and John keeps peering into my face every five minutes or so, to see if I have started yet. I can hold off for a little longer because of the tragicomedy of his concern and curiosity about me. But then I am asked to say a few words and I feel that I want to, and as I am nearly finished my voice breaks and the scene swims in front of me.

They give us a purse "to buy something for your new home." What can we buy that is worthy of five years of love and sorrow and laughter and friendship, of five years of life? And I think, perhaps a lovely lamp, for light, for light.

They come up and say good-by to us, and they shake my hand, and some of them kiss me. Some of them are embarrassed by my tears and by their own, and some are not. I have thought until my throat ached from trying not to cry of a dive into the cool water of a blue New Hampshire lake we loved as children: for years it has been the image of refreshment and dazzling coolness to which my mind turns to try and avert tears and a public scene, and it holds me for a while, but then it is no use.

A photographer has come to take our pictures for the paper. We gather up the children, and I say, "Wait a minute until my face subsides," and we all laugh a little, and I make a great busyness of arranging the children and smoothing the boys' hair and telling Mary not to squint, and I stand by Hoyt and he puts his arm around me and I press his hand against my side with my elbow and I hold my head up, at an angle I hope is becoming.

The days just before the move are not so bad, because we are so busy and we are home together and the formal farewells are over. We are eating TV dinners and finishing up the last of the peanut butter and the ketchup and the cheese, and the excite-

ment of the coming day pervades us. I am up until two the night
before moving day. Hoyt has gone to our new community for
an evening meeting with some of the men. It is a three-hour
drive, and he will stay over and come back the next morning.
When I do go to bed it is hard to sleep. I see our scene dupli-
cated in fifty parsonages around the Methodist Conference,
where families make their final preparations for moving their
life from one place to another. I think of John Wesley, two hundred years ago, charging around incessantly on horseback, trying
unsuccessfully to combine a happy home life with the driving
force of his calling. I think of the "old days," when the men
moved every year, and the more recent but still "old" days when
the men went to Conference and their wives didn't know until
they came back home several days later whether they were to
move this year or not. I think of the other times we have moved
and that this broken pilgrimage—a few years and then move, a
few years and then move—has been our lot in the past and will
be, for the rest of my husband's life as a minister. It is a guar-
anteed reminder of the insecurity of life and of our need of God.
I think of the verse from the Psalms: "Lord, thou hast been our
dwelling place in all generations." I think of people who by
choice move gaily all over the face of the earth and, wistfully,
of those who move because they have no choice but are on an
endless search for work, for health, for safety. I wonder if they
are a different breed from me, that they can stand it at all, but I
know they are not. Eventually, I go to sleep.

We are up early on moving day, and the air is charged with
excitement. The moving van rolls up to the house at 8:30, backs
heavily over the lawn, and the men come in and start taking out
our things as calmly and efficiently as though they were packing

the picnic basket and knew everything would go in. The neighborhood children gather around on the lawn and watch, speechless, as load after load of furniture is carted across the ramp between the front porch and the back of the truck. Our children go out and watch, too, occasionally offering some commentary on the pieces as they go—"There goes my bureau"; "That piano bench is pretty wobbly"—but for the most part silent spectators to the pageant.

I watch from an upstairs window as the men force the piano up the slight incline of the ramp, grunting directions to each other, nodding toward some particular recess in the dark truck where they plan to put it. It amazes me how little space the beds take up: taken apart, posts and slats and headboards, springs and mattresses piled all together, the bulk of our upstairs furniture and the arena of rest and security and sickness and love put all together in a sort of small upper loft at the high front end of the van. I think, What else is there to take up all the rest of that space, with the beds gone? But there is plenty, and it takes hours of carrying and return, carrying and return, before, cubic foot by cubic foot, the heavy contents of the van press their undiminishable bulk close to the tailgate and the open air. No space is left inside for breathing, but none is needed. For these few hours on the truck our furniture, bereft of the human spaces with which it has been surrounded, becomes again masses of matter —metal and wood and cloth—the scenery stacked in the wings before the stage is set up again.

The men are getting tired. The easy banter with which they began the day has ceased. Doggedly they wheel out the refrigerator, belted with its black canvas strap, and wheel it into place.

My husband comes back and we make our final trip through

the house. I feel detached from it already—the worn places on the wall-to-wall carpeting travel between no pair of chairs, the large unworn island in the dining room is covered by no protective table. The niches in the wall where I kept my pieces of sculpture stand ready for the object of someone else's taste. The kitchen looks somewhat as it did, and of course the bathrooms, though the linen closet door we have had trouble keeping closed swings away from dark empty shelves. Even the back yard, seen from the upper hall window where my desk had been, looks unpossessed—lawn chairs gone, clothesline down, no bicycles leaning against the garage.

The house and yard stand empty and waiting, for someone else. I hope the new family will love this place, as we have loved it—the white brick fireplace for Christmas stockings to hang against, the wonderful lightness of the house, the view of the field from the kitchen window and, farther back, the woods and then the line of low hills, the legacy of fine and friendly neighbors, the sounds of the trains going down the valley at night. Now, for the first time, I feel it is not our house any more.

We get in the car and drive most of the way to our new town. We stop for dinner along the way, and then we find a motel for the night. I do not think I have ever felt so tired. I know the worst is over. Tomorrow will be busy, and exciting, and new. Tomorrow we will begin again. Tomorrow we will be—home.

How To Marry A Minister

by Martha Hickman

Mrs. Hickman—*she married a minister*—starts her funny-serious book with some advice to young ladies who are dating seminary students as a means of capturing a minister for a husband: "If you suggest going to church on three dates in a row and he concurs, assume he is religiously insecure and will never be a minister." From there she takes off and "tells it like it is" in an amusing, entertaining and often inspiring account of what it's like to be a minister's wife.

The chapter titles alone indicate Mrs. Hickman's amusing touch. In "I Learn to Speak Methodist," she recounts the transition that she, a Baptist, made when she married a Methodist. "Gold and Myrrth and Don't be Incensed," will make you think twice about that gift you were going to give to the parsonage—what *do* you do with eight quarts of chicken gravy, and no chicken? "How To Avoid Having To Have A Dog" tells of the losing battle, starting with turtles, that she waged against a growing menagerie accumulated by three sons and a daughter. She also